TURNING
POINTS
IN EL PASO
TEXAS

☆

BOOKS BY LEON C. METZ

John Selman: Gunfighter

Dallas Stoudenmire: El Paso Marshal

Pat Garrett: Story of a Western Lawman

The Shooters

City at the Pass

Fort Bliss: An Illustrated History

Turning Points in El Paso, Texas

Desert Army: Fort Bliss on the Texas Border

Border: The U.S.-Mexico Line

Southern New Mexico Empire

Roadside History of Texas

El Paso Chronicles

John Wesley Hardin: Dark Angel of Texas

R. E. McKee: Master Builder

400 Years in El Paso

Publisher's Note: Most of the material in this book appeared first in serialized form during 1983-1985 in *El Paso Magazine*, publication of the El Paso Chamber of Commerce. We wish to thank Art Roberts, Director of the Chamber, and Editor Russell Autry who granted permission for publication here.

MANGAN BOOKS

TURNING
POINTS
IN EL PASO
TEXAS

☆

BY LEON C.
METZ

MANGAN BOOKS
6245 Snowheights Court
El Paso, Texas 79912

Library of Congress Catalog No. 85-60638
ISBN 0-930208-18-8

Design and Typography by
FRANK MANGAN

To Matthew

the last to leave

Foreword

A city without turning points is no city at all. It is a clump of buildings, a naked void upon the land.

Turning points starkly outline the past and at least dimly illuminate the future. They are the bricks and mortar of growth, maturity, judgment, compassion and strength, both cultural and economic. The shifts may be subtle or dynamic but an evolution, even if unnoticed, has taken place.

Critics may correctly argue that other turning points have been ignored. I reply only that turning points are like anniversaries, some call for bells and candles, while others are best forgotten or left to other historians.

These turning points were selected to demonstrate the twists and turns of El Paso in reaching its present accommodation with destiny. They are a common heritage, not a nobility earned but a guarantee given by right of living at the Pass of the North.

Leon C. Metz

Contents

The phrase "Silvery Rio Grande" brings a knowing smile to most El Pasoans, but this picture shot at sunset in the Pass of the North on the city's west side may shed some light on the origin of that phrase. [Photo: Cletis Reaves]

1

Big River

*The main physical circumstances of the Rio
Grande are timeless. They assume meaning only
in terms of people who came to the river.*
Paul Horgan: *Great River*

The Rio Grande is El Paso's most durable and important physical asset,
and its billion year history is the great unsung saga of El Paso. Local
residents are beholden to the river. Whether they like it or not, the Rio
Grande's turning points are their turning points.

Like many El Pasoans I grew up in another part of the country, the
Ohio River Valley of West Virginia. The Ohio I observed firsthand, but
the Rio Grande I read about only in literature, envisioning it as wide
and deep. Since authors called it "silvery," I assumed it to be beautiful
too.

I arrived at the Pass in October 1948, a seventeen-year-old airman
waiting at the Greyhound bus station for transportation to Biggs Air Force
Base. On a whim I walked south to see the river, and found the mighty,
majestic Rio Grande to be narrow, shallow and smelly.

Later that afternoon I wrote home saying, "You won't believe this,
Mom, but the Rio Grande is not as wide or as deep as Worthington
Creek. You can walk across without getting your feet wet."

That was my introduction to a river mighty in legend and powerful in
its future influence upon me.

The Rio Grande is the fifth longest stream in North America, and it means "Big River," or to quote Paul Horgan, "Great River." In Mexico it is the Rio Bravo, which doesn't translate into "brave river" so much as "wild or restless river."

Early travelers described the Rio Grande as a mile wide and an inch deep, too thick to drink and too thin to plow. Pioneers had a certain talent for poetic expression.

John R. Bartlett, the 1851 boundary commissioner, reported the river as sometimes a freshet and sometimes a roaring torrent. During portions of his first winter in El Paso, Bartlett could not cross into Mexico because of ice.

When looking south toward Mexico from El Paso's Interstate 10, the green, fertile, house-and-street covered valley that you see was formerly a river bed. The stream wasn't wide, of course, but the channel twisted and turned, overflowing, producing thickets and swamps called *bosques*. In places they averaged five miles in width.

And viewed from what is now Scenic Drive on Mount Franklin, the river and its bosque were El Paso's mesmerizing landmarks. The Chamuscado-Rodríguez Expedition of 1581 referred to them as containing lakes and lagoons.

Duck and geese darkened the sky. As late as the 1880s, El Paso newspapers mentioned trains stopping near Las Cruces, forty miles upriver in New Mexico. Passengers and crewmen shot wildfowl out of the skies with rifles and shotguns.

But how did it all start, this Rio Grande, and how did its existence become so vital to El Paso?

Geologists consider the earth's age at nearly five billion years, give or take a few million, and for most of this interval the world has been a continually changing planet. The atmosphere has writhed with dense clouds; land masses have contorted and vanished.

El Paso's geologic clock started ticking one billion years ago. Rock formations date from that period.

No one knows how frequently the warm seas swept in, but the first proven instance happened 500 million years ago. Thick limestone (seashells and fish bones) accumulated. About 250 million years ago the oceans blanketed half of North America before retreating to their present location.

As the waters slowly drained, the American Southwest evolved into swamps and savannas. What is now El Paso, Tucson, Chihuahua City and San Antonio teemed with dinosaurs and similar life forms. Dense foliage grew abundantly and flying reptiles with incredible wing spans soared through azure skies.

For whatever reason, the reptiles failed to adapt to changing conditions. The swamps and savannas dried between forty and seventy million years ago. The Rocky Mountains slowly formed. Lava pushed upward from deep within the ground, forcing a bulge in the earth. That bulge was El Paso's first mountain, born forty-seven million years ago and named Cerro de Cristo Rey, the Mountain (or hill) of Christ the King. Uplifts created the Franklin and Sierra de Juarez ranges.

Since the mountains are still rising (or the bolson is still dropping), El Paso straddles an earthquake belt. However, in spite of several small jolts in the past, the region is not considered a danger zone.

Some geologists suspect the Franklins may have soared ten thousand feet higher during an earlier age. Crazy Cat, the McMillan Quarry and Sugar Loaf are not mountains, but landslides rumbling off the original peaks. West and northeast El Paso, the Fort Bliss headquarters complex and William Beaumont Army Medical Center are built on this erosion debris.

Stripes on the colorful east face of the Franklins are the visual evidence of sediment flushed south during epochs past. The dark red lines identify soil from Socorro, New Mexico. The red clay also formed Indian Cliffs near the eating establishment by the same name at Fabens, Texas.

When the ancestral Rio Grande reached the El Paso Southwest twenty million years ago, mountain ranges blocked its exit to the sea. So it flooded natural basins in Texas, New Mexico and Chihuahua. Water reached almost to Chihuahua City and equaled Lake Superior in size. Professor Emeritus William S. Strain of the UT El Paso Geological Sciences named it Lake Cabeza de Vaca in honor of the first known European to visit this region.

Meanwhile, the earth groaned beneath the weight of silt and clay washed south from Colorado and New Mexico. Fort Bliss sits on sediment, nearly two miles deep, known as the Hueco Bolson.

With the demise of the last ice age and the melting of glaciers two-and-one-half million years ago, the lake overflowed through the Quitman Range near Sierra Blanca, Texas. Water stormed down the canyons absorbing much of the Rio Conchos channel and reducing that river to a mere tributary of the Rio Grande. The Rio Grande had now become through-flowing to the Gulf of Mexico.

Twenty miles west of El Paso, black lava bubbled from depths of

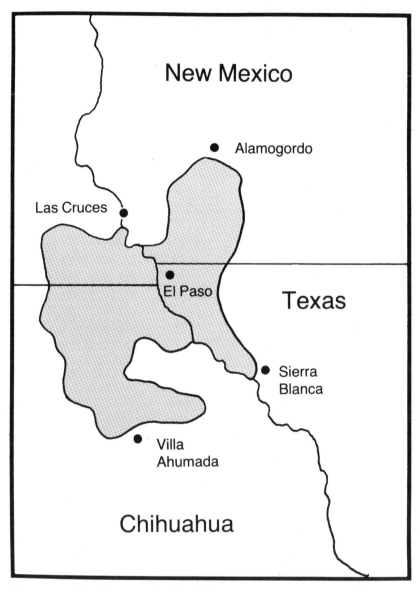

The ancestral Rio Grande reached the El Paso Southwest some twenty million years ago, but mountain ranges blocked its way to the sea. It flooded natural basins in Texas, New Mexico and Chihuahua, forming a huge lake (shown above) now known as Lake Cabeza de Vaca. Dry and wet eras caused the lake to recede or advance. With the melting of glaciers, the lake overflowed through the Quitman Range near Sierra Blanca, Texas, and the Rio Grande became through-flowing to the Gulf of Mexico. [Map: Frank Mangan]

fifty miles to violently encounter ground water locked in the river sediments. Thunderous explosions shook the land for centuries creating the volcanic Potrillo Mountains. Such cataclysms also formed Kilbourn's Hole and Hunt's Hole (named for early ranchers) and scattered miles of black basalt lava.

For a while, the river flowed between the southern extremes of the Organ Mountains and the northern tip of the Franklin Mountains, depositing sand and gravel to a depth of 1,500 feet and saturating it with fresh water. These enormous, but not everlasting, supplies awaited the human needs of the 1900s. Roughly eighty-five percent of El Paso's present water originates in this Hueco Bolson.

The river also permeated New Mexico's Mesilla Valley Bolson, those ancient deposits now in legal contention between El Paso and New Mexico. If the United States Supreme Court eventually resolves the issue, the decision may revolutionize western water law.

After flowing a few thousand years across what is today Northeast El Paso and Fort Bliss, the river changed course and cut through the narrow wall between Cerro de Cristo Rey and the Franklin Mountains. It created the imposing Pass of the North, the canyon separating the mountains. One million years ago, the river started carving the present El Paso-Juarez valley.

The Pass of the North then is a canyon, whereas El Paso refers to a river crossing, a ford in the Rio Grande on the downstream side of the canyon. Colonizer Juan de Oñate referred to the river crossing in 1598 as "El Paso del Rio del Norte," the pass (or crossing point) of the Great River of the North. El Paso and El Paso del Norte (early-day Juarez) therefore take their names from this ford.

Today the Rio Grande is North America's fifth longest river. Dams reduce its strength and velocity; pollution fouls its beauty; ditches frustrate its efforts for change; a multitude of farmers and politicians argue for its nourishment. For fifteen thousand years the river sustained prehistoric man. For the last four hundred years, it has succored the Indians, Spaniards, Mexicans and Americans. It supports a present United States-Mexico population in the El Paso area alone of over a million, and rising.

Always the river! It is the key to the past, indispensable to the future. If it were not for the Rio Grande, there would be no El Paso.

Juan de Oñate arrived at the Pass in 1598 from Santa Bárbara, Mexico. He took possession of the entire area in the name of King Philip of Spain, and brought European civilization to what would become the American Southwest. [Artist: Reynold Brown]

2

La Toma and the Right Arm of God

*Don Juan de Oñate wanted to lead some great
enterprise; carve his name deep in the hard
rock of history; rule the destinies of wide lands
and mighty peoples. We should not be far wrong
in saying that Oñate wanted to be a king.*
C. L. Sonnichsen: *Pass of the North*

Since 1540 when Francisco Vásquez de Coronado crossed the Rio
Grande near Albuquerque searching for the fabled Seven Cities of Gold,
Spain had claimed the Pass of the North by right of exploration and
conquest. But Spain *officially* pronounced ownership on April 30, 1598
when Juan de Oñate, conquistador and colonist, formally ratified *La
Toma,* the taking of possession. He did so practically inside the city
limits of modern-day El Paso.

The thrust of Spain had already shifted north from Mexico City. It
paused at San Luis Potosí, then moved on to Zacatecas, Durango and
finally to Santa Bárbara, near present-day Parral.

Santa Bárbara became the jumping off point for New Mexico, the
town being the godfather of Spanish territory north of Chihuahua. Primi-
tive Santa Bárbara mining tunnels fanned out at different levels, and the
digging was dangerous due to heavy loads, cave-ins, poor lighting and
inadequate ventilation. Since the Spanish hesitated to risk their lives,
Indian labor provided the only obvious solution. Slavers roamed the Rio

Conchos to the Rio Grande, prospecting for labor even to the Pass.

Spaniards baptized the Indians as Catholics before putting them in the shafts. When they died or were killed in accidents, the Indians went promptly to heaven and presumably were grateful for what the Europeans had done.

However, various religious orders condemned slavery and sought to convert the Indian on his home soil in New Mexico. Francisco Sánchez, nicknamed Chamuscado for his fiery beard, joined hands with three Franciscan priests led by Agustín Rodríguez. The seventy-year-old Chamuscado, in poor health, assumed charge of eight soldiers and the entire caravan.

In June 1581 the tiny but intrepid group left Santa Bárbara for New Mexico. At present-day El Paso, the expedition mentioned "lakes and lagoons" inhabited by Indians who ate raw fish. The natives were small by American standards, generally naked and tattooed. An open slot in each hut faced east, the Indians believing that some day their God would rise with the morning sun, and every home would be open to him.

Further north in New Mexico, Indians murdered the priests when, against military advice, the padres remained to preach the Gospel. All the soldiers returned safely home with the exception of Chamuscado. He died when nearing Santa Bárbara and was buried alongside the road.

After a year passed, Antonio de Espejo rode through the Pass in search of the priests. He was a wealthy man, a murderer placating the authorities by an act of religious contrition. His crimes apparently were forgiven even though he found no friars.

Nearly twenty years later, Juan de Oñate financed a major colonizing expedition into New Mexico. His father had previously discovered the silver mines at Zacatecas, and Juan in turn had developed the rich fields at San Luis Potosí. He had married the granddaughter of Cortés, the great-granddaughter of Montezuma.

But Juan was dissatisfied. He wanted to be a viceroy but settled for governor. Oñate, at his own expense, would settle colonists in wild and remote New Mexico. After all, what is a governor without subjects?

From 1595 through most of 1597, Oñate outmaneuvered a multitude of gubernatorial candidates and received Royal permission to organize his quest. He assembled four hundred men, one hundred and thirty having families. Each person itemized all personal property, especially armor and weapons. Baggage required eighty-three wagons and carts. Nearly seven thousand head of livestock added to the bedlam.

In January 1598 the expedition lumbered out of Santa Bárbara. Oñate saved months by crossing the bleak, unmapped Chihuahua desert instead of following the traditional highway of the Rio Conchos to its confluence with the Rio Grande.

For three months the caravan stumbled along the approximate path of Chihuahua's present Route 45. Traveling only as fast as the sheep and cattle, the caravan faltered. Sandals wore out. Colonists grubbed for weeds and roots. Once it rained for seven days and the wagons sank to their frames. An intense drought followed. Portions of the party split off to search for water and later described what they perceived as divine intervention. As they knelt to pray under a withering yellow sun, a deluge fell.

At Samalayuca, thirty miles south of today's El Paso, the expedition encountered awesome sand hills. Slowly the caravan lunged across, finally breaking free and reeling toward the Great River of the North, the Rio Grande.

Advance parties stampeded to the banks on April 20, 1598. Two horses promptly drowned in the swift current. Other horses drank until their bellies burst. The men gorged themselves on water, rested briefly and gorged again. When finished they lay with swollen stomachs beside the river, looking "like foul wretches stretched upon some tavern floor."

Scribes recorded the river valleys near present-day San Elizario as the "Elysian fields of happiness." They relaxed "beneath shady bowers," resting aching bodies and enjoying comforts too long denied.

When everyone caught up, the caravan trekked west along the Rio Grande to near present-day Socorro, Texas where a prayerful Thanksgiving took place a quarter-century before the one in New England. Great bonfires roasted meat and fish. Indians joined in the celebration. Mass baptisms occurred. Captain Farfán wrote a drama about natives approaching the Church on bended knee and seeking salvation. Farfán's play was the first ever performed in the Southwest.

When the festivities ended, the governor ordered everyone into ranks. Armor and weapons glistened. Then Juan de Oñate placed his hand upon the traditional Cross and took possession on the 30th day of April, 1598. In giving thanks to God, he touched all the religious bases.

> In the name of the most Holy Trinity, and of the eternal Unity, Deity and Majesty, God the Father, the Son, and the Holy Ghost, three persons in the one and only true God, who by his eternal will, almighty power and infinite wisdom, rules, directs, and governs from sea to sea, from one end to another, as the beginning

and the end of all things . . . and in honor of His most holy and venerable Mother, the holy Virgin Mary, our Lady . . . and in the name of the most blessed Saint Francis, image of Christ, God in body and soul, His royal ensign and patriarch of the poor whom I adopt as my patrons, advocates, and intercessors that they may intercede with God himself, that all my thoughts, deeds and actions may be directed to the service of his infinite majesty to increase the number of the faithful and the extension of the holy Mother church, and to the service of the most Christian of kings, Don Philip, our lord, pillar of the Catholic faith. May God grant him many years for the crown of Castile, and the prosperity of his kingdoms and provinces.

Therefore in the name of the most Christian king, Don Philip, the second of that name, and for his successors (may they be many) . . . I take possession, once, thrice, and all the times I can and must, of the actual jurisdiction, civil as well as criminal, of the land of the said Río del Norte, without exception whatsoever, with all its meadows and pasture grounds and passes.

When Oñate finished, the colonists gave a throaty shout. Soldiers fired their weapons in volleys.

What Oñate did, in taking title, *La Toma* it was called, has few parallels in history. It was as significant as the possession by LaSalle at the mouth of the Mississippi, and of Champlain at the mouth of the St. Lawrence.

According to international law and custom, with the utterance of Oñate's words, those lands watered by the upper Rio Grande passed forever into the hands of Spain. Those Indians who resisted became trespassers, lawbreakers to be dealt with accordingly.

El Paso today represents the hub of this Spanish empire, a vision enacted slightly over four centuries ago. Oñate and the right arm of God had brought European civilization to the Southwest. The Pass of the North would never again be the same.

3

Muskets at the Pass

*At the time when the nature of war is thoroughly
in flux, it is difficult to be confident about the
value of a history of the American Army.
Nevertheless, a measure of acquaintance with
the past may help to dissipate both the awe and
the contempt that alternately have hobbled
American deliberation upon military issues.*

Russell F. Weigley:
History of the United States Army

Fort Bliss is today a guardian of the free world. There was a time,
however, back in 1849, when its primary purpose was to protect El Paso
from Apaches.

The antecedents of Fort Bliss began with Colonel Alexander Doniphan and his nine-hundred-man force of Missouri Farm Boys who
reached the Pass two days after Christmas, 1846. Following their victory at the Battle of Brazito (near present-day Vado, New Mexico), the El
Paso area slipped forever from the weakened grasp of Mexico.

Looking at the El Paso Southwest from the perspective of another
century, one can find amusement in the way public figures and military
men originally perceived the region. Congressmen, and even General
William T. Sherman, suggested New Mexico wasn't worth the cost of
defending and insinuated that Old Mexico might have put something
over on the Americans when they acquired the Territory. General Phil
Sheridan complained that if he owned Texas and hell, he would "rent
out Texas and live in hell."

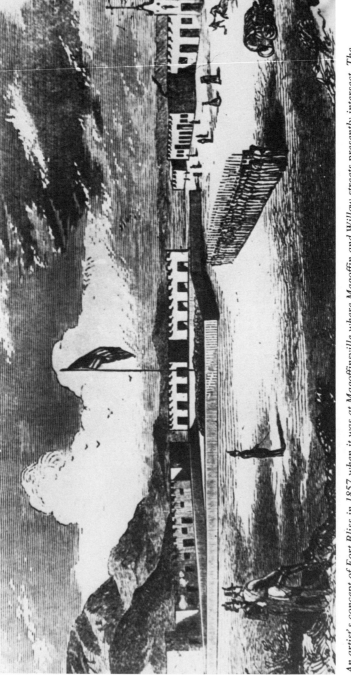

An artist's concept of Fort Bliss in 1857 when it was at Magoffinsville where Magoffin and Willow streets presently intersect. The scene is somewhat exaggerated. The mountains did not encroach that closely. The flag was probably not enclosed within stockade walls. The buildings were not likely that spread out, although they probably resembled the adobe structures shown here. The building on the far right appears to have been a model for the present replica on Fort Bliss. [From El Gringo by W. H. Davis, El Paso Public Library]

Land west of the Mississippi was considered desert, a burning cross pioneers bore in order to reach California. Few believed it would ever be settled, and certainly the soil would never be fractured by the plow. Washington sought only to protect the roads and villages.

A string of eleven adobe forts along the Rio Grande from Santa Fe south to El Paso assumed this guard duty. On November 7, 1848, the War Department issued General Order No. 58 and the Third Infantry prepared for marching toward the Pass.

Major Jefferson Van Horne took command; a slender, austere soldier graduating from West Point thirtieth in a class of thirty-eight. The forty-seven-year-old warrior left San Antonio, Texas on June 1, 1849 with 257 infantrymen, 275 wagons, 2,500 head of livestock, and hordes of emigrants. On September 8, the caravan arrived at present-day Tigua.

One-third of the soldiers occupied the old presidio at San Elizario where the Adobe Horseshoe building is now. Twenty-one miles northwest, Van Horne leased six acres for $4,200 a year. It included what is today the Mills Building west to the Greyhound Bus Station, Civic Center and Chamber of Commerce. Developer and Santa Fe trader Benjamin Franklin Coons owned the site and the area was known as Coons Ranch, or Franklin.

An assortment of adobe structures comprised the housing; buildings so nondescript that Van Horne considered them unworthy of description. He called his location "The Post Opposite El Paso, New Mexico." The El Paso referred to El Paso del Norte (Juarez), the neighboring Mexican border town of five thousand. The "New Mexico" alluded to the Post being inside the Territory of New Mexico.

West Texas ended six hundred miles east, near San Antonio. Jurisdiction did not extend to El Paso until March 1, 1850 when the 32nd parallel of latitude identified the boundary line between Texas and New Mexico, a border created by the Compromise of 1850.

At the time of its formation, the Post Opposite El Paso was the strongest military encampment in the Territory. Although its primary mission was to protect local villages from Apaches and to escort wagon trains, it also had three additional and compelling reasons for existence. It would entrench American authority firmly along the Mexican border, establish law and order, and fulfill provisions of the 1848 Treaty of Guadalupe Hidalgo. The Post would enforce Article XI and intercept marauding Indians before they crossed the international line into Mexico.

No high walls surrounded the scattered adobes, for few similarities existed between eastern and western stockades in terms of Indian warfare. Indians never attacked a single fort in the American West.

Nor were weary El Paso soldiers the stuff of popular legend. Over half were Irish or German emigrants, farmers and laborers recently off the boat and stumbling with their English. They were survivors of debtor's prisons, famine and an oppressive foreign military draft.

The recruits drilled and grew vegetables, drilled and constructed buildings, drilled and performed details. While officers generally had access to homes of the best families, the regulars had only the saloons and brothels. Punishment was brutal and life in general was tedium interspersed by dreary monotony. The government paid privates eight dollars a month, a pittance usually squandered in dives ringing the post.

Soldiers took turns guarding the plaza. They had no concept of search and destroy missions. An Indian wandered anywhere he pleased so long as he resisted all temptations to plunder Mexico and did not threaten the white man's trails.

When hostilities broke the boredom, the mobile Apaches hopelessly outclassed the foot soldiers. Troops shouldered muskets and marched many scorching miles in futile pursuit. Few soldiers ever saw an Indian, and fewer still ever shot at one.

The United States based its pre-Civil War concept of Indian warfare on the European style of mass fighting. High ranking military officers assumed that Indians should meet the regulars on a toe-to-toe basis and fire away until only the bloodied winner remained. With a few rare exceptions, the Army had no cavalry until the 1870s, for while fiction stories would have readers accepting the myths of the American on horseback, the facts were that pioneers used the horse primarily for plowing and pulling carriages and wagons. Furthermore, the cost and care of horses was an expense that neither the Army nor the government cared to assume.

In addition to chasing Indians and never catching any, the military assisted in the suppression of local lawlessness. Socorro, Texas, fifteen miles southeast of El Paso, reeled beneath a brutal assault by rowdies dismissed from the boundary service. The troubles ended when local residents and boundary employees tried four men for murder. While the Army stood guard, all four dangled from ropes in front of the Socorro Mission.

The Army proved so proficient at establishing law and order in West Texas that American outlaws fled south of the border. Mexico complained bitterly about their depredations, but a frustrated Van Horne could not get Mexican permission to cross the boundary in pursuit.

Frequently the Army saved travelers from their own folly. On one occasion sixty government wagons and a large herd of cattle stalled for fifty-six days on the salt flats east of El Paso near Guadalupe Peak. Major Van Horne rescued the caravan by placing barrels of water alongside the road.

The Post Opposite El Paso also gave assistance to United State Boundary Commissioner John R. Bartlett. Lieutenant Colonel Louis Craig and Company A escorted Bartlett between El Paso and the West Coast for two years before deserters murdered the colonel near Fort Yuma. Fort Craig, New Mexico was named in his honor.

Unfortunately, those eleven posts alongside the Rio Grande presented enormous supply problems. El Paso in particular was tethered at the end of a 1,200 mile Santa Fe and Chihuahua trail meandering in from Missouri. When the War Department reduced its budget in early 1850, Lieutenant Colonel William Wallace Smith Bliss, Adjutant General of the Western Department, appointed Colonel George Archibald McCall as Inspector General.

McCall evaluated each post in the Department of New Mexico, finding morale bad and military effectiveness worse. Only two sites had one hundred men. The Post Opposite El Paso had eighty-one. San Elizario had forty-four. Most of the officers were on extended leave and back East. Drunkenness was rampant, record keeping almost nonexistent.

McCall believed the War Department could profitably close several frontier forts, and in September 1851 the Post Opposite El Paso and the Post of San Elizario folded. The troops transferred to Fort Fillmore, near Mesilla, New Mexico.

Two years later the energetic Secretary of War, Jefferson Davis, named Colonel Joseph K. F. Mansfield as the new Inspector General and requested a fresh Southwest military evaluation. Mansfield's report is a frontier classic, on arguing for more Indian defense. His proposals led to the creation of forts Lancaster, Davis and Quitman in West Texas. He also recommended the re-establishment of a post at El Paso since Indians near there had recently been active.

Jefferson Davis ordered the Eighth Infantry from Fort Chadbourne, Texas to El Paso, and it arrived on Christmas Day, 1853. This time the troops rented quarters at Magoffinsville where Magoffin and Willow streets now intersect. On January 11, 1854, the fort officially became the Post of El Paso.

Two months later on March 8, 1854, the Post was renamed Fort Bliss in memory of Colonel William Wallace Smith Bliss who died unexpectedly. He was a brilliant officer and tactician, a soldier stopped only by yellow fever. During his brief career, he never visited El Paso. Today his remains lie on the post that proudly bears his name.

For over a century, El Paso and Fort Bliss have been friends and neighbors. In the beginning, the Post Opposite El Paso provided mail services and banking privileges. An Army band performed weekly concerts. Military contracts furnished substantial employment. Army payrolls kept the saloons and brothels busy and productive. The first Fort Bliss was a turning point for El Paso because it provided a secure military umbrella whereby a fledgling, remote community could prosper and grow.

4

When El Paso Left New Mexico and Joined Texas

*On January 3, 1850, Governor Peter Bell
nominated Robert S. Neighbors as the
commissioner to organize the western counties
of Texas. But to travel hundreds of miles across
a wilderness, much of it a desolate waste
inhabited by aboriginals, to win the allegiance
and cooperation of alien people long prejudiced
against Texas, and to wrest the region from the
maw of the United States [and the Territory of
New Mexico], Neighbors was advanced the total
salary of $500, without one cent of an expense
account.*

Kenneth Franklin Neighbours:
Robert Simpson Neighbors and the Texas Frontier

El Paso was born in New Mexico and grew up in Texas. But the city might never have abandoned its ancestral home had it not been for the Westward Movement plus tensions nudging this nation toward the abyss of Civil War.

It all began with Ponce de León's rancho, a grant of the Mexican government in 1827. By the late 1840s, Simeon Hart had built a nearby grist mill, and James Magoffin a rambling, ornate hacienda. Hugh Stephenson created Stephensonville, oftentimes known as Concordia. These isolated ranchos existed in the Mexican province of New Mexico, and along with nearby Ysleta, Socorro and San Elizario, they comprised a cluster of villages on the east bank of the Rio Grande.

Between five and six hundred miles to the east, Spain and Mexico had defined the southern boundary of Texas as the Nueces River, a stream parallel to, and north of, the Rio Grande. Texas ended somewhere west of San Antonio. In that Apache and Comanche infested wasteland, where few Europeans ever traveled, the boundaries of Texas, New Mexico and Chihuahua merged without strictly becoming identified.

Mexico had difficulty settling people in Texas, and fearing the aspirations of European powers, it invited United States colonists in as a buffer. The Americans accepted Mexican citizenship, became Catholics, intermarried, and paid their taxes and gave allegiance south of the Rio Grande. However, after the province declared its independence, General (and President) Santa Anna promptly overran the Alamo but was defeated at the Battle of San Jacinto. Victorious Texans captured Santa Anna, subjected him to uncommon duress, and forced his signature on two Treaties of Velasco. Those documents, which Santa Anna and the Mexican congress repudiated, implied a southern and western boundary of Texas as the Rio Grande *to its source,* an astonishing border that Texas historically had never possessed.

Since the Rio Grande originated in the Rockies, Texas claims included Santa Fe and the Pass of the North. The United States found the prospect perturbing, as did Mexico. A long Texas arm punching up through half a continent could seriously restrict American westward expansion. Carried to its ultimate absurdity, it could mean a Texas enlargement into California and the rise of a power capable of frustrating United States ambitions.

But belligerent Texas did not yet physically control anything west of San Antonio. To provide New Mexico with the blessings and benefits of Texas citizenship, Austin sent the "Santa Fe Expedition" in 1841. Historians still argue over its primary purpose, trade or military confrontation, and it is not beyond reason that the caravan was prepared for both. Mexico treated it as hostile, and the two forces met in bitter weather near present-day Tucumcari. The four-hundred-man column, freezing, starving and lost, surrendered. Mexican soldiers marched the prisoners to the Rio Grande and herded them downstream through Paso del Norte (Juarez) and into Mexico, an expedition ending in jails, humiliations and executions.

Meanwhile, the United States hesitated to annex Texas and risk the enmity of Mexico. When after nine years, the Americans notified Mex-

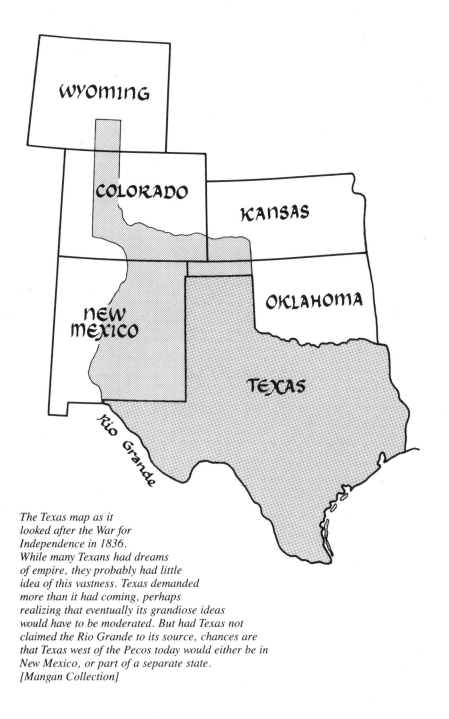

*The Texas map as it
looked after the War for
Independence in 1836.
While many Texans had dreams
of empire, they probably had little
idea of this vastness. Texas demanded
more than it had coming, perhaps
realizing that eventually its grandiose ideas
would have to be moderated. But had Texas not
claimed the Rio Grande to its source, chances are
that Texas west of the Pecos today would either be in
New Mexico, or part of a separate state.
[Mangan Collection]*

ico of impending Texas statehood, Mexico insisted that the Nueces River remain the southern border. The Americans demanded the Rio Grande, and the Nueces Strip between the two rivers became contested. When the paunchy Zachary Taylor moved troops onto the Strip, the Mexicans attacked. President James J. Polk proclaimed that American blood had been shed on American soil, and the Mexican War commenced.

While generals Taylor and Hugh Scott fought Mexico in the interior, General Stephen Watts Kearny led an army out of Missouri. It captured Santa Fe and California. Colonel Alexander Doniphan's Missouri Farm Boys split off from the main force in Santa Fe and followed the Rio Grande toward Chihuahua. Two days after Christmas, 1846, Doniphan crossed the river at Hart's Mill and peacefully occupied Paso del Norte. The north bank of the Rio Grande slipped from Mexican control and into the Territory of New Mexico.

Undaunted by a paucity of sovereignty, Texas created Santa Fe County with Santa Fe as the seat. It included not only the Pass, but the Big Bend, the Panhandle, portions of Oklahoma, half of New Mexico, two-thirds of Colorado, and bits of Wyoming and Kansas. Texas sent attorney Spruce M. Baird to establish the 11th Judicial District in Santa Fe.

Texas Governor George Wood requested United States assistance in consolidating jurisdiction. However, Washington politics being what they were, the government said one thing and the Army did another. The military refused to recognize Texas authority, saying American arms had liberated New Mexico. After two months, a frustrated Baird returned to Austin.

Texas vowed to claim its empire with a road system. Colonel John Hays, a Texas Ranger, surveyed between San Antonio and Ponce's Rancho, but became lost, wandered into Chihuahua, and was fortunate the Mexicans did not shoot him.

On February 12, 1849, Lieutenant William Henry Chase Whiting blazed a route from San Antonio through Uvalde and Del Rio to the Pass. It became the Lower Road.

Indian agent Robert Simpson Neighbors and John S. Ford, a Texas Ranger and eventual Confederate officer, surveyed a route from Austin through Fredericksburg to El Paso. It was the Upper Road.

In 1848 Ponce de León leased his rancho to developer and occasional rascal, Benjamin Franklin Coons. Coons in turn leased buildings to the "Post Opposite El Paso, New Mexico," the first Fort Bliss. The "El Paso" referred to "El Paso del Norte, Mexico," and the "New Mexico" was a reminder that the rancho was in New Mexico and not Texas.

Ponce's rancho and Santa Fe were the most prominent villages along the upper Rio Grande, although they were politically controlled by divergent groups. Anglos in Santa Fe were taciturn Northerners having little truck with slavery and almost zero sympathy or understanding for the South. The Anglos of El Paso originated primarily in Texas or other parts of the South. They were fierce, emotional believers in states' rights.

Texas, meanwhile, had no intention of forfeiting its territory. It divided Santa Fe County into four segments: Presidio (between San Antonio and the Pecos River), El Paso (from the Pecos west to include Las Cruces and Dona Ana), Worth (from near Dona Ana, fifty miles north of El Paso, to about Albuquerque), Santa Fe (everywhere else).

Austin retained the old reliable Robert Neighbors to organize the areas. Neighbors ignored Presidio County because of hostile Indians, and reached San Elizario on February 3, 1850. Since it was the largest town in the proposed El Paso County, he posted a proclamation calling for elections. Major Van Horne, commander of the Post Opposite El Paso, had no clear instructions for opposing or cooperating with Texas, so the polls opened. The vote went unanimously for Texas, and a New Mexico heritage had been repudiated. Tiny Dona Ana also voted for Texas, organizing ''splendid balls in honor of the extension of civil law.'' On March 1, 1850, San Elizario became the first county seat.

The El Paso County vote stunned federal officials in New Mexico, and they halted further elections. A judge threatened Neighbors with jail, and the organizer returned to Austin with disquieting news that portions of West Texas were in rebellion.

A series of mass meetings in Austin called for armed intervention. Governor Peter Bell asked for two regiments of mounted troops. President Millard Fillmore countered by reinforcing New Mexico. The President warned Texas that any attempt to impose civil jurisdiction by force would be resisted. In New Mexico today, Fillmore is revered for that one act of moral courage. It if were not for Fillmore, New Mexicans believe their state might now be a part of Texas.

In the meantime, Senator Henry Clay wrote the Compromise of 1850. It delayed a forthcoming civil war by a decade, and it also offered Texas $10 million to relinquish all claims west of the Pecos River. The El Paso County election would be invalid, and El Paso would return to New Mexico.

Texas balked, so Senator James A. Pearce of Maryland compromised the Compromise. El Paso had already joined Texas, so he suggested that the state's westernmost boundary extend that far but no farther. A border with New Mexico would follow the 32nd degree parallel east from the Rio Grande. The $10 million offer would stand, a figure approximating the Texas debt. This time Texas approved.

Had El Paso remained in New Mexico, it would have become the largest city. The capital might even have shifted, and certainly El Paso would have provided several governors, an achievement it has *never* accomplished in Texas.

Nevertheless, most El Pasoans believe they made the correct choice back in 1850 even though they share a mutual New Mexico suspicion of Dallas and Pedernales life styles and accents. El Paso is neither Old Mexican, New Mexican, nor completely Texan. It is a survivor, adopting the best of each.

5

El Paso and the War in the West

*After the battle it was amusing to notice with
what joy acquaintances shook hands and
congratulated each other on being alive. They
laughed and danced and shook hands with more
real joy than friends must have after years of
absence in ordinary circumstances.*

Don E. Alberts:
*Rebels on the Rio Grande:
The Civil War Journals of A. B. Peticolas*

History has relegated "The War in the West," as historians generally
have dubbed the Civil War in the El Paso region, to a few brief senten-
ces or paragraphs, as if the battles and objectives were unworthy of com-
parison with "major engagements." Yet while fighting never equaled
the massive bloodletting of an Antietam or Vicksburg, it was no less
intense, cruel and decisive. It had its own significance.

By the late 1850s, El Paso had perhaps three hundred people. Magoffinsville was three miles southeast, and Concordia a mile or two northeast of that. Two miles west of El Paso, Hart's Mill (often called El
Molino) anchored West Texas to southern New Mexico.

Texas hesitated to join the Confederacy. It voted first to secede, and
El Pasoans marked their ballots in Ben Dowell's Saloon. When the state
election went decisively for separation, Union General David Emanuel
Twiggs, a Southern sympathizer in poor health and unwilling to become
a martyr to stubbornness when so close to retirement, surrendered his

Department of Texas to state commissioners. By this act, all of the military posts in Texas, including Fort Bliss, gave their supplies and funds to state authorities. The troops had orders to walk overland to the Gulf Coast and depart by ship to the East. James Magoffin assumed responsibility for the Fort Bliss property and supplies. Simeon Hart accounted for the funds.

Fort Bliss consisted of 134 soldiers quartered in adobe buildings at Magoffinsville. Officers had the privilege of resigning and joining the South, as Lieutenant James Longstreet had done. Longstreet had been a Fort Bliss commander in 1855, and in early 1861 he brought his family to El Paso from a duty station in New Mexico and left them to await a wagon train going east. He rode ahead, enlisted with the Confederacy, and established a brilliant reputation during the Civil War.

The fiery Anson Mills opposed secession, and he urged Colonel Isaac V. D. Reeve, the commander of Fort Bliss, to move his troops to Fort Fillmore, New Mexico, forty miles north along the Rio Grande. Reeve agonized over the dilemma, but finally obeyed the Twiggs directive. Nearly two weeks before the bombardment of Fort Sumter, Reeve lowered the Stars and Stripes on March 31, 1861, and marched his units onto the rutted road leading east towards San Antonio. Soldiers from forts Quitman, Davis and Lancaster joined him along the way.

Six hundred miles east of El Paso, Texas organized two regiments of cavalry for state defense, and Lieutenant Colonel John Robert Baylor accepted command of the 2nd Regiment of the Texas Mounted Rifles. Baylor, a balding, eccentric Kentuckian had achieved notoriety during the Comanche campaigns of Texas, but after becoming Indian superintendent, Baylor resigned because of a personal policy more akin to extermination than pacification. Baylor might have then faded from public view, but the Texas Secession Convention needed someone with his homicidal tendencies to defend West Texas from Union ambitions.

Over six hundred men left San Antonio, Texas, but a few occupied Davis, Quitman and Lancaster. Elements of the Texas Mounted Rifles reached El Paso on July 3 and 4, 1861. Baylor arrived by stage. Captain Bethel Coopwood commanded a fifty man "San Elizario Spy Company," a unit consisting of riders mostly from Arizona.

The "Brigands" were close associates of the spy company and oftentimes known as "The Company of Santa Fe Gamblers." Most were New Mexico desperadoes. Like the San Elizario group, they served as spies and guides.

Between three hundred and five hundred men of the Texas Mounted

Rifles reported at Fort Bliss. While the officers usually were men of breeding, the enlisted troops frequently were scamps. A tougher, harder drinking crew had not camped at the Pass since Doniphan's Missouri Farm Boys invaded in December, 1846.

Forty miles upriver, the scraggly gray head and beard of Major Isaac Lynde made him resemble an Old Testament prophet who had neglected his prayers. He had approximately six hundred demoralized men. Conditions at the post and at Mesilla had broken Lynde's nerve, for although New Mexico was in Union territory, a ''Convention of the People of Arizona'' declared for the Confederacy, organized a representative government, and warned those who objected to leave the country. Mesilla flew the Secessionist flag openly in the plaza. The *Mesilla Times* demanded an end to Union occupation. Several of Lynde's men had ''gone south,'' joining Baylor at El Paso.

On the night of July 23, ten days after arriving at the Pass, Baylor feinted north. Two days later, believing the Federals too strong, Baylor bypassed Fillmore and occupied Mesilla. A panicked Lynde, although outnumbering Baylor, feebly attempted to dislodge him, failed, and on the morning of July 27, destroyed supplies, burned the post, and fled northeast toward Fort Stanton, 140 miles distant. The troops substituted whiskey for water in their canteens.

The Union Army stumbled ten miles to the Organ Mountains before dehydration exhausted the soldiers. Even Lynde could hardly stand, so he wearily paused at San Agustín Springs on the eastern slopes of the Organ Mountains, two miles from today's headquarters complex at White Sands Missile Range. There beneath huge cottonwoods shading crumbling adobe walls, Lynde accepted Baylor's terms and surrendered.

Forty-eight hours later, on August 1, 1861, Colonel John R. Baylor declared himself governor of the Territory of Arizona, a strip comprising the southern third of present-day Arizona *and* New Mexico. It included the Gadsden Purchase of 1853, and its two largest and most important villages were Mesilla and Tucson. Mesilla became the territorial capital.

Baylor sent Company A of the Arizona Rangers to occupy Tucson. Tennessee-born Sherod Hunter, who had lived three years in Mesilla, entered Tucson with fifty-four men on February 28. He stationed pickets to the California line.

The *Mesilla Times* published headlines screaming ARIZONA IS FREE AT LAST. However, while editor Kelley appreciated the Texas protection, he detested Colonel John Baylor. The two egotists bickered, and

Kelley criticized Baylor in the press when the colonel made contingen-
cy plans for retreating to El Paso, should an anticipated Union assault
come from Fort Craig, 117 miles upriver. The editorial implied cowardice on Baylor's part, and the colonel confronted his accuser in the
plaza. After he spat harsh expletives about the editor's ancestors. Baylor shot Kelley fatally through the head.

Baylor now turned to fighting Apaches and advocated their annihila-
tion. In a "Kill the Indians" letter of March 20, 1862, Baylor suggested coaxing the Apaches into town for a peace treaty and then slaughtering
the adults. Children would be captured and sold. However, Texas had
now joined the Confederacy, and the South wasn't as interested in fighting Indians as it was in fighting Federals. Furthermore, the War in the
West would henceforth be fought on a more professional basis. Baylor
had been an instrument of the Texas government, but President Jefferson Davis relieved him and prosecuted the New Mexico campaign with
his own choice.

Major Henry Hopkins Sibley, an ailing officer with a weakness for
the barley, had spent a majority of his military career in New Mexico
prior to joining the South in May 1861. During the next few months he
visited Richmond, Virginia and convinced Davis that New Mexico, and
perhaps the entire West Coast, should serve the Confederacy. Sibley
described Union occupation forces as feeble and incompetent, isolated
from supplies and having no support among the inhabitants. California
would easily follow a New Mexico conquest, and the Confederacy would
have a Pacific seaport, plus enough wealth to finance the war effort.

Davis believed it worth a try. He promoted the major to brigadier general and authorized a Sibley Brigade to pursue the dream.

Sibley paused in San Antonio, Texas on August 12, 1861 and awaited
supplies. Artillery and mounted volunteers arrived slowly. Sibley appointed all officers above the rank of captain. Enlisted men elected
the lower grades. Recruits furnished their own horses and usually their
own weapons. Firearms were scarce, and two companies of the 5th Regiment had lances, three-by-twelve inch blades lashed to nine-foot poles.
A crimson pennant fluttered from each. During parades, the 5th looked
like knights awaiting the commands of Scott's *Ivanhoe*. The Sibley Brigade was poorly trained and generally uneducated, but looking for a
lark.

Most of the units reached Fort Bliss in mid-December, and Sibley
created the "Army of New Mexico." He mustered Baylor's forces into
his own, and emerged with a strange yet remarkable army, one full of

scrap and vinegar, but lacking leadership and having inadequate provisions for a long and arduous campaign. Sibley hoped to supplement his shortages by living off the land and capturing materials from the enemy.

Nevertheless, Sibley could not keep his inactive army long in El Paso. It wilted under the impact of smallpox, pneumonia, dysentery and a few syphilis cases. The soldiers needed food, ammunition, clothing. Several suffered from frostbite. Replacements rarely arrived.

Sibley drank extensively, and usually was too ill for effective leadership. Colonel Thomas J. ''Daddy'' Green, a Virginian and more recently clerk of the Supreme Court of Texas, generally assumed command of field operations.

By early January, 1862, over twenty-five hundred men and fifteen pieces of artillery departed Fort Bliss and wandered past Hart's Mill, Fort Fillmore and Mesilla. They occupied the abandoned Fort Thorn, and on February 2, 1862, stood poised outside the fortified adobe walls of Fort Craig, a Union stronghold north of present-day Truth or Consequences. Green couldn't take the post by direct assault, and his cannon were too light for effective bombardment. Therefore, he assumed battle formation within sight of the Federals, flaunted the Confederate flag, and dared the enemy to come out and fight.

Inside waited a Federal force of less than four thousand, one-third being regular troops. The others were New Mexico volunteers led by Colonel Kit Carson. Colonel R. S. Canby, a cautious warrior in command of New Mexico, had no intention of accepting the gauntlet in spite of Major Sam Lockridge who boasted that if he could get a wife as easily as he could steal that Confederate flag, he would never sleep alone again. The tall, rugged Canby overruled him, making his decisions while chomping an unlit cigar.

An excuse for inaction might have come from Kit Carson who expressed reservations about the volunteers, saying they were untrained and unmotivated. Another reason might have been that the regular troops had not been paid in a year, and the volunteers not at all.

Friendship also could have influenced Canby. He and Sibley had been classmates at West Point. Canby was the best man at Sibley's wedding.

In terms of hindsight, Canby's reluctance turned out to be sound military strategy, the kind of break that sometimes comes when sound ideas and good sense are on leave. Canby had access to the Rio Grande, and he had sufficient food and ammunition. Sibley could starve while waiting for Canby to fight. With ten days of food remaining, the South had three alternatives. It could retreat, and that was unacceptable. It could storm the walls of Fort Craig and be destroyed, and that was equally unacceptable. Or it could simply circle the fort and proceed north, in the process leaving an armed camp at its rear. Option three had only limited merit, but it was better than one or two, so Sibley prepared to bypass Fort Craig.

Here again, he had two possibilities, neither pleasant enough to make his day. If he circled west, his wagons ran the risk of bogging down in sand. If he circled east, he had to ford the murky, icy Rio Grande to avoid the Fort Craig cannon. Even after reaching the opposite bank, he would have to cut a road north for twenty miles before recrossing the river at Valverde.

Green made it to the east bank without serious mishap and struggled north without water because the Rio Grande was undrinkable. A number of thirsty mules stampeded back to the ford and were rounded up by Federals. That mule loss was a costly blunder. The Confederates abandoned thirty wagons due to a shortage of animals.

Canby sent infantry and artillery to intercept Sibley at Valverde, and on the evening of February 21, both armies clashed. The Union suffered 68 killed and 160 wounded, the Confederates 36 dead and 150 wounded. Sibley retired due to his traditional illness, while Green ordered cavalry and infantry against two Federal artillery positions. Canby repulsed one, but the second overran Captain Alexander McRae's battery, capturing six cannon and killing McRae, a popular figure in El Paso. McRae Boulevard is named in his honor.

Green might have severed the Federal lines of retreat, taken prisoners and even doubled back and captured Fort Craig. None of this happened because right at the moment of defeat, Canby unfurled a flag of truce. During the ceasefire, both sides regrouped and buried their dead. When the truce ended, the Federals hustled safely back to their barracks.

Sibley captured Socorro after a brief battle, and left over a hundred sick and wounded at the hospital. Then a cold, hungry and weary Army of New Mexico headed for the closest source of available supplies, the Federal military depot at Albuquerque.

To the Confederacy's dismay, Canby outflanked it with express riders who arrived hours ahead of Sibley. A starving Southern army reached Albuquerque just in time to watch the supplies burn.

But the Confederate luck held. Southern sympathizers at Cubero, sixty miles west of Albuquerque, captured a small Union depot stockpiled with materials for Indian campaigns. And at Carnuel Pass, fifteen miles east of Albuquerque, Confederate soldiers seized thirty-three relief wag-

Left above: Confederate Colonel John Robert Baylor can be likened to an inmate in charge of the asylum. His homicidal tendencies made him a good man in a fight, but he was an embarrassment to his peers after the bodies had been removed. [Arizona Historical Society]

Right above: General Henry Hopkins Sibley wanted the Southwest and the West Coast for the Confederacy. The complex, tormented Sibley had a checkered career, and his inept invasion of New Mexico was not one of the highlights. [U.S. Military Academy Archives]

At right: Federal General Edward Richard Sprigg Canby had barely a trace of great military leadership. In 1862 he was a cautious warrior in command of New Mexico. A good reason for his inaction at Fort Craig may have been that his troops were unmotivated, regulars had not been paid for a year, and volunteers not at all. [U.S. Military Academy Archives] ons headed for Fort Craig. A desperate situation had been temporarily relieved.

On March 10, Santa Fe easily fell, and except for isolated military pockets such as Fort Craig, Sibley controlled New Mexico to the California line. The only remaining prize was Fort Union in the northeastern part of the Territory, *the* major supply post for the Department of New Mexico and West Texas. With its capture, the conquest would be complete except for mopping up. Even Fort Craig would have no option except to surrender as it could no longer be supplied.

From Santa Fe, Sibley turned toward the mountainous Glorieta Pass and Apache Canyon, fifty miles distant, the gateway to Fort Union. The general expected a leisurely trek and an easy capture, not realizing that Colonel John P. Slough and the 1st Regiment of Colorado Volunteers (called "Pike's Peakers" by the Texans), had reinforced Fort Union and moved to engage the South. Along with Slough rode Major John M. Chivington and 418 cavalrymen. The chubby Chivington would became infamous a decade later for the slaughter of Black Kettle's people during Colorado's "Sand Creek Massacre."

The Battle of Glorieta Pass began at 10:30 A.M. on March 27, 1862. In the absence of Sibley, attending to "administrative" matters in Albuquerque, Lieutenant Colonel William Read "Dirty Shirt" Scurry took command. When Slough marched to the entrance of Apache Canyon and failed to enter, the balding Scurry went after him. Six hours later it was all over. The "Gettysburg of the West," as some historians colorfully describe it, had been decisively won by Southern arms. Scurry lost thirty-six men, the Union, fifty.

But while the two armies fought, Major Chivington slipped behind the distracted Texans and struck their rear like a thunderbolt, burning the Confederate supply train. At the apex of an amazing victory, the South suddenly was denied food, clothing and ammunition.

Sibley ordered a withdrawal to Albuquerque to await supplies from El Paso, materials that never left San Antonio. To make the situation more grim, Canby had finally emerged from his lair at Fort Craig. By April 12, Sibley buried several cannon and abandoned Santa Fe and Albuquerque. Canby seemed content to harass him from opposite the Rio Grande, dropping occasional artillery rounds among the Confederates as a reminder to keep moving.

When the retreating Sibley reached Fort Craig, a defiant Kit Carson blocked his way. The post was still too strong for assault, so Sibley ordered his remaining supplies burned, his soldiers to march across one hundred miles of treacherous, nearly waterless mountains. It became a desperate every-man-for-himself ordeal.

The trek of death lasted eight wretched days, and the trails were occasionally littered with bodies and equipment. Only seven wagons remained, and when the survivors at last re-emerged alongside the Rio Grande near Rincon, they lacked even a fighting spirit. Their only remaining ambition was to shoot Sibley. Over one hundred had been killed or died during the last few months. Nearly five hundred had been taken prisoner. Dozens resembled skeletons. The soldiers practically collapsed upon arrival in the Mesilla Valley, their scrubby and pathetic bivouacs scattered randomly along the Rio Grande nearly to El Paso.

Now the Pacific Coast added its contribution to the Civil War. The two-thousand man California Column led by the cold-eyed Colonel James Henry Carleton, moved relentlessly through Tucson, driving out Captain Sherod Hunter and his scouts. By late May, Carleton approached Mesilla, and Sibley's remaining forces straggled back through El Paso and on to San Antonio and Austin, never to threaten West Texas and New Mexico again. The Confederates left twenty-five sick and wounded in the Fort Bliss hospital. A daring endeavor had come to a despondent end.

The California Column placed El Paso under martial law. Union soldiers camped near Hart's Mill. The twenty-five Confederates were treated, paroled and sent home.

Late-night curfews went into effect. Travel required a military permit. Civilian law gave way to military courts. Although El Paso was spared the severe effects of Reconstruction, the village resembled a ghost town. Empty buildings decayed everywhere.

El Paso had been a thriving, prosperous village until the turning point of the Civil War. With hardly a shot fired, the city was destroyed. Its merchants, practically all of whom supported the South, had fled, their property auctioned for nickels from the plaza. Only the coming of the railroads two decades later gave El Paso a new sense of life and destiny.

As for the careers of those Civil War generals, they did not end at El Paso. Carleton replaced Canby as commander of New Mexico. In 1865 Carleton lifted martial law and kept the Indians under control. He studied natural science and made numerous contributions to the Smithsonian, including a 632 pound "Carleton Meteorite." On January 7, 1873, at the age of fifty-eight, he died of pneumonia.

Edward Richard Sprigg Canby was transferred east following the War in the West. He became a major general in the regular army, captured

Mobile, Alabama, and soon afterwards received the surrender of generals Richard Taylor and Edmund Kirby-Smith, the latter commanding the last Confederate army in the field. In 1870 he headed the Department of Columbia, and attempted to negotiate a settlement of the Modoc War. On April 11, 1873, while unarmed and in a northern California conference with Indian representatives, Canby was murdered by Captain Jack, the Modoc leader. The general was fifty-six.

Henry Hopkins Sibley returned to central Texas following the New Mexico debacle. In December 1869, he became brigadier general and chief of artillery in the army of Khedive Ismail I of Egypt. After returning to the United States in 1874, he lectured on Egypt while seeking royalties for the "Sibley Tent" he had invented prior to the Civil War. Sibley died in Fredericksburg, Virginia on August 23, 1886. He was seventy.

Today, well over a century after the War in the West, it nearly defies belief that so much blood, agony and futility could have occurred in such a brief period. So many intrepid paladins fought and died in a struggle that affected the outcome of the Civil War not one iota.

6

Blood and Salt

The Salt War, like all wars, was wasteful and
unnecessary, unless to prove to a pessimist that
men can die bravely in a bad cause.
C. L. Sonnichsen: *The El Paso Salt War*

By the 1870s, El Paso County, without planning to, had segregated itself along racial lines. The older towns of Ysleta (the county seat), Socorro and San Elizario, had been predominately Mexican for centuries.

El Paso, however, had been an "American" community since the 1840s. It had few people, but it possessed economic clout, the army post of Fort Bliss, and most of the political muscle.

By standards of the time, the valley villages and El Paso were separated not only by miles, but by vast differences in culture, religion and tradition. Each was an entity practically within itself, and all were ill-prepared when their worlds collided in the bloody turmoil history calls the El Paso Salt War. When it ended, over a dozen people were dead, and two racially different groups had reached a belated but necessary conclusion that they needed each other.

For centuries the Mexican people had gathered salt from beds ninety miles east of El Paso within the shadow of Guadalupe Peak. Those are the same salt flats that people drive through today in air-conditioned comfort while enroute to Carlsbad Caverns from El Paso.

During the 1870s, convoys of two-wheeled ox carts groaned to the lakes from towns on both sides of the Rio Grande. Drivers shoveled the salt onto floorboards, the water drained off, and the mineral was sold for a few coppers a bushel.

The salt was free, but the trade was so brisk that El Paso politicians attempted to claim the land and charge a fee for every bushel removed. W. W. Mills, Albert J. Fountain, Gaylord Judd Clarke, A. H. French, Ben F. Williams and J. M. Lujan became the "Salt Ring."

Leadership of the ring fell to William Wallace Mills, the collector of customs. Mills later wrote *Forty Years in El Paso,* insuring that he would have the last word on practically every controversy, and he had a lot of them. His creation was an inspired (Mills called it one of the ten great books of the Western World), if at times awkwardly phrased, account containing inaccuracies as well as astute observations and chronicles of his ringing hatreds.

Mills cooperated with Louis Cardis, a former captain in Garibaldi's army in Italy. Cardis reached El Paso from Italy in 1864, and could have easily carried the title as the most immaculate politician in town. He identified with the Hispanic grievances, and became their *patrón* (patron or boss). Mexicans trusted him and generally followed his advice when voting.

Mills and Cardis also shared a common connivance with Father Antonio Borrajo, the parish priest at San Elizario, a stoop-shouldered padre said to have "salt beds on the brain." Borrajo hated Americans almost as much as he loved money, but he kept his dislikes silent while he schemed with his partners and urged his people to pay the fees.

The conspiracy might have continued indefinitely had not several Salt Ring participants engaged in rivalries. Mills and Fountain split along personal and political lines, with Fountain going off to Austin as a state senator. Mills brooded in El Paso, and then published corruption charges in the newspapers against Fountain.

When Fountain finally cleared his name, he formed the "Anti-Salt Ring," taking Gaylord Judd Clarke and Albert French with him. Clarke became the El Paso district judge, and French was appointed captain of the State Police.

On December 7, 1870, events moved from talking to shooting. Fountain walked into Ben Dowell's saloon on El Paso Street (the entrance to the present-day Paso del Norte Hotel), and encountered attorney Ben Williams busily depleting the liquor supply. A fight started with Fountain raining his walking stick down upon the head of Williams, and Williams drilling a couple of minor six-shooter holes in Fountain's best clothes.

It ended with Williams going home and barricading the door, and Fountain going home to bleed and get his rifle. He told Clarke and French what happened, and they attempted to batter down the attorney's door.

Williams took a shotgun, slipped out through a window, and killed Clarke. At that time, Fountain arrived, and he with his rifle and French with a pistol managed to shoot down Williams.

Fountain looked over the grisly scene, and decided this might be a good time to leave town. He moved to Mesilla, New Mexico, founded a Republican newspaper, fought A. B. Fall during some titanic political struggles, and became a strong, unyielding force for law and order. Twenty-six years later, he and his eight-year-old son Henry were slain near today's Highway 70 entrance to White Sands Missile Range. The unsolved killings are still New Mexico's greatest murder mystery.

After the killing of Ben Williams in 1870, a lull awaited the 1872 arrival by stage of a Missouri lawyer named Charlie Howard, a Democrat so unconventional that he did not drink whiskey. He, Cardis and Borrajo not only agreed on the salt beds, they supported each other's political aspirations. Howard became district attorney and then district judge. Cardis went to the state legislature.

As sometimes happens in partnerships, however, the strong become contemptuous of the weak. Differences arose regarding the salt beds, the splitting of profits, who actually owned what, and what each other's respective roles should be. Howard turned against Cardis, and beat him brutally with his fists on the streets of Austin and San Antonio.

Borrajo's anti-Americanism now roared into the open, his caustic tongue becoming such an embarrassment that two bishops ordered his removal to a parish across the Rio Grande in Guadalupe. That was fine, except that Borrajo refused to go. Bishop J. B. Salpointe came by buggy from Tucson to ease Borrajo out in a gentle fashion, but found himself blocked at Socorro by the priest and his angry supporters. Borrajo called the good bishop a "Protestant" and other vile names. Nevertheless, Borrajo, submitting to Church authority, reluctantly changed his parish.

In the meantime, Howard claimed that several attempts were made on his life. On one occasion a mob in Ysleta dragged him through the streets, took him to San Elizario and forced him to sign a paper vowing "to forget all that had happened" during the last few days. Howard also promised to leave the country and never return. The courts would decide who owned the salt beds.

Once back in El Paso, Howard ignored the agreement and went gunning for Louis Cardis, blaming his former ally for all his misfortunes. With a shotgun, Howard chased Cardis into the Solomon Schutz store on San Francisco Street (where the Greyhound Bus Station is now), and killed him with two blasts. Sheriff Charles Kerber said Howard did a fine thing.

Major John B. Jones of the Texas Rangers arrived to restore order by organizing a local group of Rangers. Several were wanted outlaws in the Territory of New Mexico, and should have been in jail instead of acting in the capacity of police officers. Even so, Jones chose an honest captain in John B. Tays, a brother to Reverend Joseph W. Tays of the Episcopal Church. John Tays had integrity, but that was about all. In terms of leadership capabilities, he possessed hardly a trace.

As Major Jones returned to Austin, Charlie Howard and approximately twenty Rangers rode into San Elizario on December 12, 1877. They had planned to enforce Howard's ban on salt unless the fees were peacefully paid, but on hand to argue was a sullen, threatening crowd of armed men. Within hours the rangers were under siege. Local storekeeper Charlie Ellis tried to reason with his longtime Mexican friends, and was murdered.

Sergeant C. E. Mortimer stepped outside a building in which the Rangers had taken refuge, and was slain by an unseen rifleman. For the next forty-eight hours the lawmen underwent constant attack.

"Boys, I will surrender," Howard said. "It is the only way to save your lives." With that he passed around his money, wrote a few messages, and turned himself over to the Mexican contingent. A bully was now redeeming himself through courage.

With Howard in custody of the rabble, Tays surrendered the Texas Ranger company, the only time in history that such an event ever happened. The officers were stripped of their weapons and locked up.

From across the river, Father Borrajo allegedly sent instructions. "Shoot the Gringos and I will absolve you."

The mob led Howard to a vacant lot and a firing squad, but the executioner performed so sloppily that the wounded man fell into the dirt and thrashed about. Horsethief Jesús Telles ran forward with a machete, took a wild swing as Howard twisted away, and watched in amazement as two of his own toes flip-flopped through the air.

Two of Howard's friends, John Atkinson and Charlie McBride, were dragged out next. Again the squads had to reload twice to completely kill each man. The bodies were stripped, mutilated, and pitched into an abandoned well.

The mob looted San Elizario and disappeared into Mexico. Although an El Paso grand jury indicted six, nobody went on trial.

Another group of "rangers" became vigilantes. They rode through the valley with a wagonload of coffins, extracting a bloody revenge. At least a half-dozen Mexican males, and one woman, were indiscriminately shot by the marauding Anglos.

What were the results of the Salt War?

After a congressional investigation that took reams of testimony, Fort Bliss was reactivated. If Fort Bliss had been there during the international outbreak, those final executions and murders might never have happened.

Of even greater consequence, the Anglos of El Paso and the Mexicans of the valley towns reflected on what their ethnic racism had brought them. Both sides had plenty for which to be ashamed, and as the wounds healed, each realized the importance of cooperation, understanding and responsibility. The Salt War ended by becoming a turning point for humanity at the Pass of the North.

No. 246 prepares for an 1882 departure from the Santa Fe Depot in El Paso. No turning point in El Paso history has proven more significant than the arrival of the railroads. [Leon Metz Collection]

7

Lonesome Whistle

*By the third anniversary [in May 1884] of the
coming of the first railroad to El Paso, the City
of the Pass had become one of North America's
major rail centers. What a few years earlier had
been a small, sleepy, and extremely isolated
adobe village was now a fast-growing small city
with rapid and dependable freight and
passenger transportation to every major
population center on the continent.*
                        Edward A. Leonard:
                Rails at the Pass of the North

No event in El Paso's history ever brought such spectacular and
dramatic growth as the railroads. In the spring of 1881, the Southern
Pacific became the first of four lines to enter the Pass of the North.

By 1880, El Paso had approximately seven hundred people working
for the military, the saloons, or for wagon masters along the Chihuahua
Trail. While the town could proudly call itself the Gateway to Mexico,
and could brag about its importance to the Butterfield Trail, the bottom
line was that few travelers ever paused except to re-outfit and drink a
warm beer. With vibrant economic expansion and development, all created by the railroads, El Paso had a runaway population of over ten thousand in less than a decade.

The Atchison, Topeka & Santa Fe rolled south through New Mexico,
spinning its steel rails across the inhospitable *Jornada del Muerto,* the
Dead Man's Route. From central Texas, the Texas & Pacific laid track

at almost a mile a day toward El Paso, as did its affiliate, the Galveston, Harrisburg & San Antonio. The Mexican Central built from Juarez to Mexico City, and it is still the longest line in Mexico. It also remains today the only line from Mexico City to the American border. A spur extended across the river into El Paso.

Out in California, the Southern Pacific hurried east, the workers struggling and straining, sweating and blasting, carving narrow niches in the close-grained rock, each day getting a few more rails and a few more ties closer to El Paso. Chinese coolies shoveled across half a continent from San Francisco Bay. By March of 1880 they were in Tucson.

As the Southern Pacific approached, El Paso residents listened to the nighttime explosions from the Chinese encampment. Skyrockets lit up the darkness as the Chinese brightened the monotony of their lives.

Crews laid tracks across what is now City Hall and the Chamber of Commerce building. They swept down the center of Main Street alongside the Public Square (San Jacinto Plaza). This placed the lines so far north that no one believed the town would expand that far. However, within two years the community had leapfrogged the tracks, and newspapers were calling for the removal of those rails because they blocked traffic and impeded the city's growth.

The Southern Pacific arrived on May 19, 1881. The engine steamed across the Fort Bliss parade ground (Hacienda Cafe area), and halted probably near what would later become the St. Regis Hotel, now a historic parking lot.

Charles Crocker, of the Big Four of San Francisco financiers, and president of Southern Pacific, exited first. He was followed by Colonel Bean, superintendent of the Tucson Division, and W. E. Brown, president of the Southern Development Company. Everybody gathered in a makeshift tent pavilion where El Paso Judge Allen Blacker, in splendid oratorical style, repeated what politicians said all over the country when the railroads came to call. He expounded on the glories of unlimited growth: "His Excellency, the Governor of Texas, said to me only last winter," Blacker insisted, "that if he were a young man, he would settle in the valley of El Paso, with the firm belief that it would be within his power to become a millionaire — that El Paso is the best place in the United States to make a fortune in a single lifetime."

Don Espiridon Provencio spoke for Juarez, assuring the officials that "Mexico, my country, salutes and congratulates you today." The long procession then walked down San Francisco Street to Schutz Hall where the ladies awaited.

James P. Hague, who had donated thirty acres for railroad right of way, had no peer as an orator, and always sounded good even when nobody understood what he was saying. "The Lone Star, in the splendor of her course," he intoned, "shall now enter the portals of the Golden Gate; the Nereid of the Pacific shall now add to the wealth of her dominion, the chief jewel that once adorned the diadem of the Montezumas."

The audience suspected that it had just heard something profound, so it vigorously applauded.

Residents and visitors today find it difficult to comprehend the stupendous effect that the 1881 railroads had upon old and modern El Paso. Railroads completely transformed a lifestyle and culture. El Paso as it presently exists would be impossible to imagine had it not been for the railroads.

They removed El Paso forever from the age of isolation. The Chihuahua Trail, the wagon trains and the stagecoaches swiftly became obsolete.

The railroads attracted businessmen like Charles R. Morehead and O. T. Bassett. Although Fort Bliss had a post office and bank which civilians used, the rails brought such rapid prosperity that civilian banks swiftly became a natural course of events. Morehead and Bassett established the State National. Adolph Schwartz built the Popular Dry Goods.

El Paso soon had gas, water (of sorts), electricity, telephone service. There was an ice plant, a school, a fire department. Trinity Methodist Church went up. Providence and Hotel Dieu hospitals started. *The El Paso Times* and the *El Paso Herald* began operations. Farmers finally had a market outside of the narrow El Paso valley.

The railroads turned El Paso into a center for the performing arts, since the town was a comfortable stopover between large cities. The Nellie Boyd Dramatic Company played frequently, as did Edwin Booth and Lawrence Barrett. The latter gave stirring renditions of *The Count of Monte Cristo* and *Julius Caesar*. John Barrymore, Sarah Bernhardt, and Harry Houdini played to substantial audiences, Houdini hanging from a high wire in Pioneer Plaza.

John L. "I can lick any man in the world" Sullivan, "Gentleman Jim" Corbett, Peter Maher, and Bob Fitzsimmons were just a few prize-fighting champions, or near champions, who boxed exhibitions in the downtown area. Several nationally recognized wrestlers performed.

Rails brought the gunfighters and the shady ladies. Fully six hundred Chinese remained in El Paso after the railroads departed. Chinatown existed from present-day Mills to Fourth Street before condensing in a downtown region south of Overland. El Paso maintained a recognizable Chinatown until World War II.

Railroads changed the face and complexion of El Paso as developers and builders shifted from adobe to lumber and brick. The city struggled to resemble other American communities.

Consumptives arrived, and housing failed to keep pace. Railroad and Chamber of Commerce publications vividly described the curative health benefits of El Paso's desert climate. Tents extended down several streets. More tents dotted Highland Park. Tiny houses with sun porches mushroomed where Southwestern General Hospital is today. The Vendome (Cortez) Hotel catered to "lungers" who relaxed on west side balconies and took advantage of the afternoon warmth.

El Paso became the southwestern center for Mexican and American mining activities. The ASARCO smelter started in 1887, solely because the railroads could furnish a continuous feed of copper ore from Mexico and Arizona.

Of far greater significance, however, railroads made possible the Mexican Revolution on a massive and bloody scale. Rails accounted for the swift and vast movement of armies, for whoever controlled the railroads essentially controlled the country. Thousands of refugees took advantage of the rails to leave Mexico and settle in El Paso. Hundreds spent months in empty downtown boxcars because they had no place else to go.

The majority of El Paso Hispanics trace their local roots directly to the 1910-1920 revolutionary era. They fled conflagration and brutality south of the border.

Today, even though historians speak glowingly of El Paso's four-hundred-year history, they date the city's progress and growth from 1881. There have been many turning points since, but none more far-reaching than the one on May 19, 1881 when the railroads came to town and forever vanquished the frontier.

8

The Case of the Stolen County Seat

*The election date [for a county seat] was set for
December 3, 1883, and the ward heelers went
to work, Ysletans confident of victory.
Unfortunately for their cause, El Paso came up
with more "wards" than did Ysleta, principally
because enthusiastic El Pasoans crossed the
river into the precincts of Paso del Norte and
granted United States "citizenship" to many of
their Mexican friends for election day.*
John Middagh:
Frontier Newspaper: The El Paso Times

The El Paso boosters in 1883 faced a difficult problem. They had to
convince a majority of county residents that El Paso was the city of the
future, that it deserved the county seat. There were two ways to accom-
plish this, and both would be tried. They would wage a broad campaign
with emphasis on the justice of their cause, and they would instigate the
first known fraudulent election in local politics.

The struggle for the seat started in 1850 when southern New Mexico
abandoned its heritage and joined Texas. El Paso County formed in
March, with San Elizario as the largest village and the first county seat.
In 1854 the seat briefly shifted to Magoffinsville, then little more than
a ranch. The move suggests either financial turmoil, or an effort to seek

the military protection of Fort Bliss. Magoffinsville held on for only a month or so, and then the seat returned to San Elizario.

Ysleta won the county seat in 1866 but a tenacious San Elizario promptly regained it. Finally in 1873, Ysleta again wrested it from San Elizario, establishing in the process a courthouse and county offices. The law even hanged a man for rape, and there are few indications of political potency more chilling and impressive than a good hanging.

Twelve miles upstream, the city of El Paso coveted the seat. Until 1881, it was merely an adobe, remote village across the Rio Grande from El Paso del Norte (present-day Juarez). The presence of the largest city on the Mexican side of the border practically guaranteed that its Texas neighbor would be equally large and influential, but El Paso had additional advantages which ultimately prevailed over its Texas neighbors. Three newspapers flourished in 1883. El Paso was a gateway into and out of Mexico. It had two banks and a post office. Furthermore, it was predominately Anglo, it had economic clout, and it successfully lured the railroads. (Ysleta also shared in the Southern Pacific.)

Ysleta could keep the county seat for five years, and three had already lapsed. With El Paso rapidly expanding because of the railroads, however, the town might outgrow, and thereby outvote Ysleta by 1885. Ysleta could either safely wait two more years and risk losing the seat, or it could call an immediate election and retain the seat for another five years.

The petition for election had 109 signatures, many from El Paso. A thirty day campaign started, and Simeon Newman, bombastic editor of the *El Paso Lone Star,* led the fight. He called Ysleta "a wayside railroad station that would never amount to anything," and described El Paso as representing "enterprise, wealth and energy," a community "leaving its adobe past behind for the iron and brick of the future."

El Paso newspapers accused the county judges of being unable to speak English, an unfair charge since fourteen out of the first twenty judges (1850-1883) were Anglos, several from El Paso. Of the six Mexican-Americans, each had roots in the county's oldest families and likely spoke better English than some of their counterparts. However, the support staff, miserly paid and poorly trained, had language problems.

The El Paso Times criticized the Ysleta courthouse as tiny and inadequate. Ysleta had no hotels or creditable eating houses. A couple of days spent in Ysleta on county business drained the finances and punished the body.

The *Times* identified El Paso as the county's commercial and business center, and said "our natural and geographic position demands" the seat. The federal government had promised "a magnificent and imposing public building" if El Paso won. "Valley lands, now worth only $5 or $6 an acre, will increase to $50 and even $100 and $150 an acre," reported the *Times*. "Your tablelands will have artesian wells and will be dotted with herds of cattle worth millions."

El Paso committees made the arduous and expensive trek to Socorro, San Elizario and Camp Rice (early Fort Hancock) to politically twist arms. Meanwhile, Ysleta seemed lackadaisical and overconfident.

A remarkably quiet election day arrived in late December. Most of the saloons closed. The *Lone Star* reported less than a half-dozen drunks, and no wild shooting.

The voting favored El Paso by almost five to one, 2,366 votes to 535 votes. Concordia voted fifty to zero for El Paso. Socorro went for El Paso 124 to 46, and San Elizario by 118 to 59. Camp Rice gave all forty-three votes to El Paso. Ysleta captured only its own precinct, 426 to 3.

El Paso, with between three and four hundred eligible voters, mustered an incredible 2,034 turnout. Four of those voted for Ysleta, possibly because someone did not use the pencil string. The string had one small knot. By placing the knot along the top edge of the ballot and pulling the string tight, the pencil marked exactly where it was supposed to. The practice assisted those unfamiliar with the English language.

None of the newspapers expressed moral outrage, the *Lone Star* being especially smug. "They say on the street that the Mexican vote will be the largest ever polled in El Paso," Editor Newman stated a week or so before the election. "Mexican citizens are becoming as interested as El Pasoans in having the county seat."

In fact, Juarez furnished over half of El Paso's voting strength. Owen White, El Paso's first historian, claimed Mexican residents were paid in proportion to the number of ballots they cast. Over a thousand men crossed the border and performed their civic duty. Politicians paid them at the corrals and at Chopin's Hall, the latter within sight of the courthouse.

Several Americans voted irregularly too. W. D. Wagner, who returned to El Paso thirty-three years after the election, claimed he voted three times and "didn't feel ashamed." The Ysleta people were "no babes in the woods," he explained in justification.

Owen White mentioned a prospector who walked into El Paso on election day and found a Mother Lode. First, he voted in each of the three

Above: El Paso's first county courthouse was a grand, ornate edifice graciously centered in a "park" offering shade trees and walkways for strollers or business people. [El Paso Public Library]

Below: El Paso's present county courthouse, completed in 1916, wraps around the first courthouse which was subsequently razed to make way for Liberty Hall. [J. E. Morgan Collection, UTEP Library]

precincts. Then he trimmed his whiskers and made the rounds again. Next he sported only a mustache, and on the fourth and final trip, he showed up clean-shaven. Altogether he voted twelve times and left town with cash in his pockets plus a new suit of clothes for his public services.

Ysleta raised not even a perfunctory complaint. County Judge Marsh Rogers, commissioners González, Armendariz and Julian, plus Sheriff James H. White abandoned Ysleta overnight. One can surmise only that they were closet supporters of El Paso. They held their first commissioners court meeting in El Paso's city council chambers, and passed a resolution asking Governor John "Ox Cart" Ireland to turn the old courthouse into a school. Today the structure is gone, but Ysleta Elementary sits on the foundations.

Commissioners rented the Auzerias Building in El Paso for $35 a month, and it became the county jail. County officers occupied the Hague and Hills Building, at San Antonio and Mesa streets, and the Catron and Fewel Block, where San Antonio intersects El Paso Street.

The election turned El Paso into a political and economic powerhouse by regional standards. The population jumped from eight hundred in 1880 to over ten thousand in 1890. The *Times* said El Paso would "build a courthouse grand, magnificent and costly, unsurpassed by any other county building in Texas."

When El Paso erected a courthouse where Liberty Hall is now, charges of fraud stunned the county. The structure was indeed "grand, magnificent and costly," a monument to greed as well as vision.

After the election, editor Newman called for an "El Paso rule so honorable that all will love it, so free that none will feel it, and yet so strong that all will fear it."

That's not exactly how newspaper editors would express it nowadays, but it reflected a prevalent view of the time. At any rate, El Paso had the railroads, the military, the political clout, the economic potential, and now the county seat. Soon it also had a burgeoning population.

Whether or not the county realized that an era had passed, no one can say. The written record is silent, but the political, cultural and economic repercussions linger on. The county seat led El Paso into the 20th century.

9

The Struggle for Law and Order

*At a busy intersection of South El Paso Street
and West San Antonio Avenue in downtown El
Paso, a bronze plaque affixed to the wall of the
venerable Hotel Paso Del Norte reads: FOUR
MEN IN FIVE SECONDS. Near this spot on
April 14, 1881, four men were shot to death at
almost the same instant, and newspapers in
places as far away as Santa Fe, Kansas City,
and Chicago hit the streets with headlines which
screamed, "Bloody Battle," and "War Raging
in El Paso."*

Fred R. Egloff:
El Paso Lawman: G. W. Campbell

Slightly over a century ago, El Paso, Texas retained a hired gun to enforce its ordinances. And so began the bloodiest twenty-four months in community history.

In a sense, law and order arrived in 1850 when San Elizario became the first county seat. The sheriff's office was a hard twenty-one mile ride from El Paso. The law's jurisdiction also extended in the opposite direction several hundred miles to Presidio. Furthermore, the county seat constantly changed locations between San Elizario, Magoffinsville and Ysleta.

The Texas Rangers assisted with law enforcement, but they were stationed at the county seat at Ysleta and patrolled El Paso only when asked, and then only briefly. As for Fort Bliss, it struggled to prevent desperados from plundering Mexico and seemed uncertain about how it should handle private vendettas in Texas.

The city had recently consisted of four isolated ranches: Hart's Mill, Ponce's Rancho, Magoffinsville and Concordia. The centrally located Ponce's Rancho became El Paso in 1859. With five railroads approaching in 1880, their impending arrival attracted a reckless and transient population. "Imagine the main street of San Angelo, Texas," Judge Pruess said upon returning to that village, "with all the houses flat roofed, and about a thousand drunken men, railroad hands, gamblers and adventurers, all swaggering, fighting and yelling through the streets and you have a pretty good idea of El Paso as it is."

The town incorporated in July 1880, and El Paso Street was the alameda, a tree-lined boulevard. Chihuahua, Oregon and Santa Fe streets went north and south. San Antonio and Overland streets extended a block or so east of El Paso Street. San Antonio Street led toward Ysleta and on to San Antonio, Texas, while San Francisco twisted toward Mesilla and on to California. The business section comprised everything south of Pioneer Plaza. Today's San Jacinto Plaza was the Public Square, a dump for trash and manure. The caliche streets often resembled arroyos when savage summertime thunderstorms sent relentless streams of water thrashing down from the Franklin Mountains. A mule-drawn street car rattled between El Paso and El Paso del Norte (Juarez). On the eve of the arrival of the railroads, the Texas town had seven hundred people.

Mayor Soloman Schutz and six aldermen appointed John B. Tays as the first marshal in July, 1880. His greatest moral strength was a blood relationship to Parson Tays, the respected pastor of St. Clements Episcopal Church. His greatest moral weakness was a lack of leadership during the El Paso Salt War three years earlier. Tays was the only Texas Ranger commander who ever surrendered to a mob.

Nevertheless, it was road repair that undermined Tays. The council ordered him to smooth a hole on San Francisco Street, and he filled it with trash. Unimpressed by this engineering, the mayor dismissed Tays on October 25.

A. I. Stevens, a forty-seven-year-old mechanic who repaired wagons and carriages, replaced Tays as marshal. The council appointed Bill Johnson as deputy. In a village tolerant of hard liquor and wicked ways, Bill Johnson was the town drunk.

Stevens assessed and collected taxes in addition to jailing lawbreakers, but the council removed him on November 26 for "neglect and dereliction of duty." The minutes revealed no details.

Kentuckian George Campbell now took a turn. He was a capable, articulate officer, a former deputy sheriff of Clay County, Texas, and a recent city marshal at Las Vegas, New Mexico. With a big grin, he accepted the badge in early December 1880, a week or so short of his thirtieth birthday. Bill Johnson remained as deputy.

The city did not pay a salary but a percentage of fines. If a judge assessed three dollars, the judge kept a dollar, the city took a dollar, and the marshal collected a dollar. Of course, if the judge imposed no penalty, or if the defendant had no money, the marshal received no compensation.

Mayor Solomon Schutz acted as municipal judge as well as the town's leading merchant, which meant that criminals frequently best able to pay were the ones most often set free. The mayor treated them as voters and potential customers.

Campbell insisted upon a modest salary to supplement the fees. The city refused although it offered amends by requesting Texas Rangers to assist the marshal. Two days before Christmas, with Campbell present, the administration drafted a plea to Governor Oran Roberts:

> We the mayor and Board of Aldermen . . . to better adminis-
> ter the law and city ordinances, [believe] that the time has now
> come when . . . we are unable to protect life and property. And
> the reasons for such inability we respectfully assign the following:
>
> 1st. That the sheriff of this county and his deputies . . . reside
> fifteen miles distant.
>
> 2nd. A Marshal and his Assistant Marshal, together with one
> Constable, constitute the police force of this city. The force is
> not stronger for the want of funds . . . to provide compensation
> for police officers, and to maintain the municipal government.
>
> 3rd. The Southern Pacific and the Rio Grande and El Paso
> Railways are on the eve of completion to this point. As the fore-
> runner and followers of such enterprises, we now have turned
> loose upon us hordes of vagabonds, gamblers, burglars, thieves,
> and particularly murderers.
>
> 4th. Like classes have also poured into El Paso, Mexico [Juar-
> ez], one mile distant . . . and thus one place is a refuge for crim-
> inals and fugitives of the other. We have no doubt that in each of
> the El Pasos, confederates for crime are now being formed, with
> aides and confederates in the other.

Therefore, to the end that law may be enforced, peace and good order preserved, and life and property protected, we respectfully request that Colonel George W. Baylor and his detachment of State forces [Texas Rangers] now stationed at Ysleta, be ordered here for the purpose of aiding the municipal authority until such time as the municipality shall be able . . . to execute the law and its ordinances.

Governor Roberts ordered the Rangers into El Paso but the city refused to furnish quarters. The angry Rangers camped near the present-day Coliseum, a site remote from downtown. Campbell asked to be relieved.

The council had the request under consideration when armed thugs celebrated New Year's 1881 by roaming the streets and firing shots at the moon and into the homes of Schutz and the aldermen. If Campbell did not encourage the riot, he at least made no effort to suppress it. When the Rangers arrived the next morning, they chased several hooligans out of town.

The council and Mayor Schutz believed Campbell should have better preserved the peace. Campbell disagreed, and as tempers heated he turned on his heel, walked onto El Paso Street, drew his six-shooter, and challenged the mayor. A frightened Schutz sent deputy Bill Johnson and a couple of Texas Rangers to arrest Campbell, charging him with assault and attempted murder. The officers sympathized with the marshal, and chuckled when Campbell scribbled obscenities across the warrant and then spat on it. When the warrant returned to Schutz unserved, the mayor hysterically protested to Baylor.

Baylor asked his Rangers why they had not enforced the law. The two replied that Campbell was a personal friend, and they believed his position in the controversy to be correct. Without comment, Baylor discharged them.

Baylor ordered Ranger Sergeant James B. Gillett and Corporal George Lloyd up from Ysleta to arrest Campbell. By this time, however, Campbell had gone to the Hale Ranch near Canutillo, ten miles north of El Paso. The thirty-five-year-old John Hale was born in Iowa and grew up in California. During the Civil War, Hale helped occupy El Paso with the Union's California Column. When the conflict ended, he remained at the Pass with his wife Angelita, five daughters and one son. His ranch became a notorious rendezvous for stolen cattle driven from Mexico over what is now Fort Bliss and northeast El Paso. The livestock crossed through Smugglers Pass, where today's Trans Mountain Highway cuts through the Franklin Mountains, and hid in the Canutillo bosque. Hale employed renegade Texas Rangers, and he gave refuge to Campbell. Since the marshal's absence from village affairs seemed to quiet the mayor's fears, the city dropped charges on January 14, 1881, and accepted Campbell's resignation.

On the day Campbell quit, the council swore in Ed Copeland, owner and operator of the Occidental Saloon. Copeland was promised $50 a month, plus arrest fees, but a new ordinance required a $500 bond. When he couldn't raise the money, the city dismissed him a month later.

In despair the council now turned to deputy Bill Johnson, appointing him temporary marshal. For the first time the city sought a professional gunman, and a six-foot-four killer wearing revolvers in leather-lined hip pockets answered the call.

Green-eyed Dallas Stoudenmire arrived by stage from Socorro, New Mexico where he had been city marshal. He was born in Alabama, fought in the Civil War at fifteen, and migrated to Columbus, Texas where he killed two men. His brother-in-law, Samuel M. "Doc" Cummings had opened the Globe Restaurant on El Paso Street. Doc encouraged the thirty-five-year-old Stoudenmire to seek the marshal's vacant position. Dallas did so, and was sworn in on April 11, 1881, the sixth marshal in eight months. Although the newspapers mentioned "discrepancies in his $500 bond," nobody complained, for the officer with his big six-shooter and his "belly-gun" with its sawed-off barrel, looked every bit the unrelenting killer that the city fathers wanted.

The council handed Stoudenmire his badge and told him to get the jail keys from Bill Johnson. The marshal found Johnson intoxicated, and stripped the keys from his pockets. He then viciously shook the deputy and discharged him.

Although the marshal now had enemies he didn't need, he was unaware of other events, the consequences of which would soon engulf him. Seven Americans had robbed an inebriated Juarez merchant and were jailed in Mexico. When no trials started, señoritas smuggled guns into the prison and a jailbreak erupted on February 18, 1881. Frank Thompson shot a guard and dashed for the river. Four others followed. The Lafayette Kid stumbled and lay in the street until police re-arrested him. Pat Ryan paused in a nearby saloon, had a drink and surrendered peacefully.

Thompson, J. C. Cain and Frank O'Neal almost made it. They reached an *acequia* (irrigation ditch), their last barrier to the Rio Grande, and were treading water when a lone vaquero killed them. Officials tied the bodies to burros, dragged them through the streets and buried them in a ditch.

Six weeks after the killings, and only one day after Dallas Stoudenmire took office, Mexican rancher Ynocente Ochoa complained to Colonel Baylor that thirty head of cattle had been rustled. Ochoa suspected Johnny Hale. Baylor sent Rangers and vaqueros to investigate, but in the heavy underbrush they found only three steers, all of whom Hale swore he had purchased. The Rangers seemed satisfied and returned to camp. Only two vaqueros remained, one of them being the young slayer of the three desperados in the irrigation ditch.

Late that afternoon, vaqueros Gilberto Juarique and José Sánchez paused under a tree to smoke. At that moment, former Texas Rangers Chris Peveler and Frank Stevenson murdered them. The slayers claimed the cowboys had stolen horses and were shot while fleeing.

On April 14, fifty armed Mexicans rode into El Paso from Paso del Norte and milled around the office and store of Mayor Solomon Schutz near San Francisco and Chihuahua streets. Over Stoudenmire's vigorous objections, the mayor gave permission to recover the bodies. El Paso constable Gus Krempkau acted as guide.

That afternoon the Mexicans and their grisly cargo returned, stopping at Judge J. A. Buckler's office on the west side of El Paso Street at what is presently the West San Antonio intersection. Krempkau interpreted at the inquest.

Outside, armed Anglos grumbled that Mexicans had no right to carry weapons in town. A shootout seemed likely until merchant Ben Schuster talked Judge Buckler into sending the Mexicans and buckboard, plus contents, into a less exposed position on South El Paso Street.

Meanwhile, Buckler abruptly dismissed the inquiry without indictments. The Mexicans went home. Marshal Stoudenmire strolled to the Globe Restaurant, passing a window sign reading, ''No flies, dust or noise.'' A few minutes later, shooting started.

Ex-city marshal George Campbell had stood in the dust of El Paso Street and bitterly criticized Krempkau, accusing him of slanting his courtroom translations in favor of the Mexicans. Hale sat brooding in a narrow adobe window with deep insets that traditionally reached to within a couple of feet from the ground. Campbell bitingly turned from Krempkau, and reached toward a withered tree branch and the reins of his horse. As his arm moved upward, Hale drew a pistol and shouted, ''I'll take care of this for you, George.'' He fired.

Krempkau staggered but drew and gamely sprayed the street with gunfire. A bullet struck Campbell in the foot. Another wounded Hale.

The constable collapsed as Stoudenmire dashed from the Globe Restaurant. Seeing Hale leaning against an adobe pillar, the marshal drew his long-barreled revolver and attempted to put him down permanently. His first shot dropped an innocent bystander. Undeterred, Stoudenmire snapped off another round. The bullet struck Hale in the forehead, killing him instantly. By now the street had become a confused mass of scrambling bystanders, dying men and rearing horses. Nearby Texas Rangers dodged for cover. A struggling Campbell, who had not even pulled a weapon, screamed, "This is not my fight!" The marshal thought otherwise, and shot him.

Stoudenmire's first bullet broke Campbell's right arm. His second slug buried in Campbell's stomach, the gunman falling, writhing in agony, and gasping, "You big son of a bitch, you murdered me."

A coroner's jury found Dallas Stoudenmire properly "executing his duties." Authorities ignored the innocent bystander. In happiness at retaining such an uncompromising law-and-order man, the city started paying the marshal $100 a month, plus fees. It also awarded him a gold-headed walking stick, the epitome of prestige.

But some residents grumbled. Several believed Campbell had been murdered. Friends of Hale and Campbell prevailed upon Billy Johnson to get revenge for the thoughtless manner in which Stoudenmire had humiliated him as a deputy. They encouraged Johnson to blow away the shame with gunpowder.

On Sunday evening, April 17, 1881, six days after Stoudenmire took office and three days following the bloody gunfight, Johnson waited with a double-barreled shotgun at the northeast corner of San Antonio and El Paso streets. The State National Bank (now MBank) was under construction at its first location, and a neatly piled stack of bricks fronted the building. Johnson climbed on top and waited for the marshal to make his rounds.

Stoudenmire walked north on El Paso Street as darkness approached. Beside him strolled Doc Cummings. When the distance between the lawman and the ominous holes in the shotgun narrowed to a few yards, Johnson fired both barrels . . . and missed. Stoudenmire and Cummings returned the fusillade, slamming eight bullets into Johnson. A combination of bad whiskey and oozing blood soaked through the bricks and into the sand.

As a postscript, the community buried Bill Johnson where the downtown public library is today. Many years later, when the city moved the

Dallas Stoudenmire (standing) City Marshal of El Paso in 1881. The two gentlemen seated are Neil Nuland and J.W. Jones, proprietors of the Acme Saloon. (It is an interesting sidelight that gunfighter John Wesley Hardin was gunned down in the Acme Saloon in 1895.) Stoudenmire became involved in a personal vendetta with the Manning brothers in El Paso resulting in a bloody street fight which cost him his life in 1882. [Rose Collection, University of Oklahoma]

cemetery, several buddies pried off the casket lid. Johnson looked better than they did. Then before their astonished eyes, his body turned to dust.

But as the former deputy died at the intersection, bushwhackers across El Paso Street opened fire on the marshal. Their aim wasn't any better than Johnson's, and instead of the marshal running for cover, he and Cummings charged and drove the attackers off.

During the bedlam, a bullet nicked Stoudenmire in the heel, and a colorful string of profanity did nothing to ease the pain. Once the excitement died down, he could barely walk, so he limped to a buggy and rode to the Ranger camp near Ascarate to recuperate. In his absence, a squad of Rangers patrolled El Paso.

During the interim, Doc Cummings organized vigilantes, the only known Committee ever to function in El Paso. It lasted a week or ten days, and several participants planned to rake one particular saloon with rifle and shotgun fire. However, other members objected, calling the action murder because railroad hands and laborers slept on the floors, benches and chairs. When a majority refused to risk slaughtering non-involved parties, the Committee dissolved in recrimination. It would never again be a factor in El Paso's struggle for law and order.

By the first part of May 1881, Stoudenmire resumed his preoccupation with terminal law enforcement. Had he used more discretion and made peace with the Texas Rangers, who should have been his natural allies, he might have prevailed. Instead he created a law and order paradox.

Stoudenmire had confidence in Sergeant James Gillett and Colonel Baylor, and appointed Gillett as chief deputy. He harassed the other Rangers, suspecting with some justification that many were former New Mexico outlaws. He considered the Rangers "untrustworthy and unreliable, more ready to aggravate than preserve the public peace." He called them cowards, accusing them of running "most ingloriously when called to the scratch." This last charge was probably a reference to the gunfight when four men died in five seconds. Stoudenmire thought the Rangers should have assisted. Instead, they did the natural thing and dove for cover.

The three Manning brothers aroused his hatred. George Felix "Doc" Manning was a short, feisty physician and an accomplished violinist. Frank had a bar in the El Paso upper valley, but he sold it and purchased the Ben Dowell place where the present Hotel Paso del Norte is located. It became the Manning Saloon.

James Manning opened the Coliseum Saloon and Variety Theater at El Paso and First streets, a block or so south of the Manning Saloon. It looked like an adobe barn but it had a large stage and several private boxes.

In the meantime, Doc Cummings and a Kansas sheriff trailed a rapist into Chihuahua. In February 1882 Doc returned only to find Stoudenmire and Gillett ill with the flu. As Stoudenmire recovered, he visited Columbus, Texas and married Isabella "Belle" Sherrington, a former sweetheart. In the marshal's absence, Doc imagined himself the only bona fide officer in town. First, he vowed to clean out the Coliseum Saloon and Variety Theater, so he blustered into the bar, ordered a drink and taunted Jim Manning into having one too, knowing that Manning was a recovered alcoholic. As the two argued, Doc became more abusive, threatening to "let Manning's light out," and repeatedly asking if Manning "was fixed" (armed).

According to Manning's story at the inquest, he had shunned trouble until a showdown could no longer be avoided. As Doc sipped a drink, Jim accepted the challenge, and Cummings drew late. His bullet hit the plastered wall as two bullets hit him. Doc staggered through the batwing doors, fell in the dust of El Paso Street, groaned loudly, and died.

The State charged James Manning with murder but never brought him to trial. He was the only person indicted even though his revolver contained but one empty chamber. Bartender David Kling probably fired the other shot. To make matters more mysterious, Doc had a fracture across the top of his head. Someone, most likely Kling, clubbed him before he died, perhaps even before he drew.

When Dallas Stoudenmire returned with his bride, Deputy Gillett met him at the depot with the sad news. At this point, the feud between him and the Manning brothers became a raging obsession with Stoudenmire. The marshal drank heavily, became more argumentative, and during one spree set up targets and re-enacted his "Four Dead in Five Seconds" shootout. It was clear warning for the Mannings.

The marshal soon became as irresponsible and dangerous as the town hoodlums, so the *El Paso Lone Star* printed an editorial entitled "Law and Order" on March 25. "The citizens of El Paso are standing on a volcano," it stated. While the newspaper mentioned no names, editor Simeon Newman obviously had the marshal and the Mannings in mind. "Our Streets may be deluged with blood at any moment and it is with the object of arousing people to this fact that these lines are penned. Violence if allowed to break forth can only have the effect of paralyzing business and driving people from the city. Now is not the time to discuss the right or wrong of past issues.'' The editor continued, ''Tale bearers and agitators must be made to understand that their services are not wanted and their interference will not be permitted.'' The editorial pleaded for ''cool heads, stout hearts, and a clear understanding.''

The column brought action. On April 16, the *El Paso Herald* published a peace treaty.

> We the undersigned parties having this day settled all differences and unfriendly feelings, hereby agree that we will meet and pass each other on friendly terms, and that bygones shall be bygones, and that we shall never allude to any past animosities.
>
> Signed
> Dallas Stoudenmire
> James Manning
> George Felix Manning
> Frank Manning
>
> Witness
> R. F. Campbell
> J. F. Harrison
> F. V. Hogan
> J. P. Hague

The truce merely placed the hostilities on hold. It permitted the marshal to concentrate his vexations elsewhere after the city elections ended.

Joseph Magoffin, a pioneer landowner and businessman, became mayor. His father had been James Magoffin, founder of Magoffinsville. Joseph took office on August 30, 1881, and one of his aldermen was Noah H. Flood, a former district attorney in San Francisco. Flood thought he should advise Stoudenmire on legal matters, but the marshal thought otherwise and drop-kicked him through an open doorway.

Another enemy was William Wallace Mills, better known as W. W., and a brother to Anson Mills, who had laid out the street system of El Paso in 1859 and had even named the town. As the new mayor and aldermen took office, Mills submitted a petition calling for Stoudenmire's removal and a Mills appointment. The ploy might have worked, but Stoudenmire submitted an even longer petition asking that he be retained.

A few weeks later Mills accused Stoudenmire of becoming a United States deputy marshal. The city office was declared vacant, and Alderman James P. Hague, a witness to the Stoudenmire-Manning peace treaty, nominated Mills for marshal. Alderman Ben Schuster nominated Dallas Stoudenmire. The council deadlocked and Mayor Magoffin broke the tie by supporting Stoudenmire.

Nevertheless, the marshal's drunken onslaughts were becoming an embarrassment to a council not easily embarrassed. Aldermen hoped an ordinance forbidding public officials from drinking might be a solution. They adopted the following resolution on December 10, 1881:

> Any officer of El Paso, who within the limits of said city be guilty of drunkenness, shall be fined not less than ten nor more than one hundred dollars.

A list of municipal employees followed. Stoudenmire's name fell a considerable distance down the column.

Feeling righteous over all the abolished sin, the aldermen also made it unlawful for a male to carry a gun, fight, drink, gamble, swear, disturb the peace, expose himself indecently, or be ''seen in the company of a known prostitute not his wife or some other relative.''

By now, Stoudenmire had little support left. He antagonized parishioners by using the St. Clements church bell for target practice. Sometimes he drunkenly treed the town. On occasion he bellied-up to a bar, drank himself unconscious, and spent the night sleeping on the hardwood floor.

His accounts were constantly out of order, while deputy James Gillett submitted almost perfect records. For three months the marshal received no salary because he spent unauthorized funds. When Magoffin offered to straighten out the files, Stoudenmire growled that he had been ready to settle for weeks, and the mayor had been putting him off. The *Lone Star* hinted that the money had financed Stoudenmire's frequent bouts with the demons.

Editor George Washington Carrico of *The El Paso Times* said the town had little crime during Stoudenmire's periods of sobriety. When Stoudenmire was drinking, however, the crime rate soared. Stoudenmire threatened to run Carrico out of town.

Meanwhile, the peace treaty gradually dissolved, and the *Lone Star* published an editorial aimed at the mayor and council:

El Paso Street looking toward Juarez from the balcony of the Grand Central Hotel, location of today's Plaza Theater. The famous Newspaper Tree is on the left; San Francisco Street begins near lower right. This view (circa 1880) shows El Paso as an adobe community. Between the two sets of horses and wagons is 1881's Four Dead in Five Seconds gunfight location. City Marshal Dallas Stoudenmire died in the same area in 1882. [Aultman Collection, El Paso Public Library]

This scene, from the same location on previous page, dates from about 1885. The adobe buildings are gone, but the Newspaper Tree still stands. The mule car tracks come up from Juarez. A concrete sidewalk lines the left side. In spite of progress, however, animals still have the right of way, and wagons still remain the favored mode of transportation. [Aultman Collection, El Paso Public Library]

The citizens of El Paso look for you to avert . . . the danger to the peace and prosperity. Already the cloud that has been hanging over the community has seriously damaged every branch of business; and an actual outbreak will retard the city a year in its growth. The dullness of business at the present time is in great measure due to the fact that many people have heard of the troubles here, have been deterred from coming, and not a few who were here have left. The council can, by doing its duty, avert disaster and revive business. Their duty is to make a proper investigation of the question, to do this with open doors, and then remove or reinstate the marshal. If he has not done his duty, or if his continuance in office is a threat to the peace, he ought to be removed. Public policy dictates that, even if a man be a good officer, if he is obnoxious, or if his continuance in office is liable to provoke serious trouble, perhaps even a riot, he ought to be removed. Let the council act with a high sense of public duty and quit dilly-dallying.

On May 27, 1882, the council met to discuss Stoudenmire, all of the aldermen preferring the safety of open windows rather than the comfort of sitting at a table. Alderman Flood even entered through a window, cautiously placed a shotgun outside but within reach.

Alderman Phillips did not attend. Since Stoudenmire had threatened to shoot him on sight, his absence was not considered strange.

The aldermen discussed the issue in closed session, then invited the marshal inside. Stoudenmire walked in twirling a six-shooter, and stopped in front of Flood. "I can straddle every God-damned alderman here," he snapped. Magoffin cleared his throat and adjourned the meeting.

Two days later on May 29, Stoudenmire sobered and submitted his resignation. "While I have suffered an injustice from certain members of your honorable body," his letter stated, "I beg to assure you that I meant no disrespect to you or the people who you represent."

After accepting the resignation, Alderman Hague praised Stoudenmire's "faithful service." Other resolutions did likewise. Then the council appointed Deputy James Gillett as the new marshal.

Six weeks later the federal government swore in Dallas Stoudenmire as a United States deputy marshal with headquarters in El Paso. He returned from Deming on September 17, 1882, and for a few minutes sought a wanted man in the Manning Saloon. Not finding him, Stoudenmire wandered down to South Utah Street (now South Mesa) to Cora

Bell's brothel. From the yard he drunkenly called for his favorite, Carrie. She had left for a bite to eat, so Dallas waited in the parlor until Carrie returned from her "lunch break."

When he re-entered the streets at 10 o'clock the next morning, the Mannings were armed and waiting. Someone said Stoudenmire had sought them in their saloon the night before.

Stoudenmire growled that he could whip the brothers all at once or one at a time, but he sought only a wanted criminal without success. Emissaries carried that explanation to the Mannings, all of whom seemed relieved to hear it, except Doc. Frank and James especially wished to avoid a confrontation, as each had premonitions of death. After several hours of negotiations, all parties gathered in the Manning Saloon to shake hands and sign another treaty.

The crowded Manning Saloon was a scene of cordiality. Doc Manning played billiards as Jim chatted with a customer near the bar. It might have been a gathering of old friends.

Stoudenmire ordered a drink and asked for Frank. "I'll go find him," Jim said, and left.

Doc Manning approached the bar and Stoudenmire said something about a bunch of liars causing trouble. "You are the liar," Doc snapped.

Both men reached for their guns as a mutual friend pushed them apart. That well-intentioned act cost Stoudenmire time. Off balance, he drew last. Manning's first shot smashed Stoudenmire's left arm, severed an artery, entered the chest, bounced off a rib and exited through the breast. The marshal's belly-gun fell heavily onto the wooden floor.

The doctor fired again, the bullet striking Stoudenmire in the shirt pocket but not penetrating the skin due to a wad of wanted bulletins plus a photo of an unidentified woman. The impact knocked the marshal through the doorway and onto El Paso Street.

As Doc Manning rushed outside for the kill, Stoudenmire got off a shot from his other pistol. His slug hit the physician in the arm, and the doctor's gun spun into the dirt. Stoudenmire now possessed a clear advantage, but was badly wounded, bleeding profusely, and struggling to cock the revolver one more time with both hands. Doc did not wait. The physician, perhaps five-foot-six, rushed the tall man, wrapping himself tightly around Stoudenmire's arms.

A waltz of death started along the sidewalk; Stoudenmire desperately trying to shake the doctor loose, the doctor just as desperately hanging on. At this moment, James Manning ran up, saw the struggle and aimed his .45 at Stoudenmire's bobbing, weaving head. The first shot missed and shattered a barber pole. The second struck the marshal behind the left ear. Stoudenmire collapsed, the doctor falling atop him, wildly clubbing the former city marshal with his own weapon.

James and Doc Manning went on trial at the county seat of Ysleta for murder and were acquitted. The foreman of the George Felix Manning jury was W. W. Mills. Ike Blum was on the jury that acquitted James Manning, and he had been a partner in Jim's saloon business. All of the Mannings subsequently left town. Frank died in the Arizona State Hospital in 1925. Doc Manning practiced medicine in Flagstaff, Arizona and died during the same year. James Manning became a wanderer, dying in 1915 in Los Angeles. He is buried in Forest Lawn.

Dallas Stoudenmire lay in the street with hardly a dime in his pockets. El Paso Lodge No. 130 of the Freemasons paid the funeral expenses. Coffin lumber cost $4.50, a suit of burial clothes, $11.55. He was shipped to Columbus, Texas and all efforts to locate his grave have failed.

James Gillett wrote *Six Years with the Texas Rangers,* one of the finest and most authoritative books of its kind. But as the El Paso city marshal, he was not without faults. His wife, the daughter of Colonel Baylor, divorced him for adultery. The marshal clashed with mayor pro tem Paul Keating, a saloon owner. Gillett unwisely accused Keating of drunkenness. Keating claimed Gillett collected fees and taxes without properly accounting for them. An enraged Gillett struck the alderman and threatened to shoot him. The council dismissed Gillett, and he retired to a ranch near Marfa and Alpine, Texas where he organized the world famous Cowboy Camp Meetings. He died in 1937.

Although the marshal's office rarely functioned smoothly even after Stoudenmire and Gillett, the city had made a credible turning point away from lawlessness. The six-gun and the frontier faded into history. The outlaw and the quick-shooting lawman had reluctantly yielded to civilization.

10

Shady Ladies

If there was no demand—or need—for their
services, the prostitute would not exist. It's as
simple as that.
H. Gordon Frost: *The Gentleman's Club*

Brendan Francis once wrote, "Since time immemorial, prostitutes have been the reward of men of action — soldiers, sailors, cowboys, gangsters — because whores are, above all else, women of action. Talk is not their stock in trade."

And so it was in old El Paso. The problem was that arguments over prostitution so divided the community that men of goodwill could not always come together and settle other long-term burning issues.

No doubt there were numerous Indian, Spanish and Mexican ladies who warmed the tents of conquistadors, but according to Gordon Frost's history, *The Gentlemen's Club: The Story of Prostitution in El Paso,* the first recorded shady lady to reach town was Sarah Borginnis, better known as the "Great Western." This attractive Amazon arrived in El Paso shortly after the Mexican War, and operated a small "hotel" near what is now the Plaza Theater. Later she drifted to more comfortable pastures in Arizona.

For the next thirty years a lack of transportation delayed the arrival of many American girls to the Pass, and it was not until 1881 that the Southern Pacific steamed into the community. Overnight the population zoomed from a few hundred to a few thousand.

El Paso extended from San Jacinto Plaza south, and encompassed roughly what is now downtown. Utah Street (nowadays South Mesa), between Overland and Paisano (formerly Second Street) had ornate parlor houses, and these specialized in attractive girls in fancy clothes sitting on garish furniture. They sold expensive sex, and were managed by the Big Five of El Paso madams: Etta Clark, Alice Abbott (better know as "Fat Alice"), Gypsie Davenport, Tillie Howard and May Palmer.

Prostitution flourished for approximately fifty years, and the city controlled it with $5 fines per girl each month, a form of licensing. Officer Pat Powers collected. Most of the money went for police and fire department salaries and expenses.

First efforts at reform began in 1885 when churches and ladies groups complained that the practice of sin should be abolished from the "decent" portions of town. The city council agreed, and cleared El Paso Street from the Plaza south to today's Paisano Drive.

A year later when the city increased its fines to $10, over 150 prostitutes marched on city hall and demanded more respect. A near riot was averted when the mayor and council threatened to investigate each girl for any non-payment of past fines. The rebellion fizzled.

By the mid-1890s, El Paso had an estimated six hundred prostitutes. To control their activities, an ordinance created a specific area known by many colorful terms: Tenderloin, Reservation, District and Zone of Tolerance. The region included East Overland from Oregon to Utah (now Mesa), south on Utah to Third, west on Third to Oregon, and north to Overland, the point of origin. Council ordered all "working" girls immediately onto the reservation, and forbade their leaving for any purpose whatsoever. They could not enter the "decent" section to shop, go to church, visit relatives or friends, or even seek medical attention.

Few girls wanted that much control over their lives, so for six months they bribed officers to look the other way. The mayor and council quickly tired of the game, however, and on July 27, 1890, fired the entire police department.

Meanwhile, additional El Pasoans believed the city should become even more strict with prostitution. The Women's Christian Temperance Union vowed on February 20, 1900 to fight the practice, and they conducted a torchlight parade through the tenderloin, suffering crude indignities in the process as moralists often are prone to do. Then to their dismay, the city government took all their petitions and recommendations under advisement, and forgot about them. The reform effort momentarily collapsed.

Nevertheless, a start had been made toward morality, and when Mayor Joseph Magoffin, considered a little *too* friendly toward prostitutes, declined to run again in 1901, the reformers fielded B. F. Hammett, who won the race. However, except for talk about closing the saloons on Sunday, not much happened.

Then in the fall of 1902, Albert Mathias, a wholesale dry goods merchant doing business at the corner of Utah and Overland, handed a petition to the city council calling for the abolition of the tenderloin. Although it bore only thirty signatures, those included a majority of downtown businessmen and property owners. On February 4, 1903, the reservations closed even though the word unofficially spread that if the brothels moved south to between Seventh and the Rio Grande, no restrictions would be placed on activities. Unfortunately, this area was already densely populated with "cribs," their dutch doors swinging constantly. So while a few girls transferred to the new zone, most stayed where they were.

This set the stage for the mayoral contest of 1903 between reform candidate and former sheriff, James H. White, and the president of the State National Bank, Charles R. Morehead. White was the most popular, and ordinarily would have easily won, but the town had already suffered through as much reform as it could stand. It disliked the prospect of additional disruptions, and preferred a candidate walking a more moderate line between the two extremes. Morehead was elected, and on June 6, he rescinded the former ordinance and reopened the reservation.

Nevertheless, reformers continued to believe they had sin on the run, and would eventually prevail. Following a thunderous downtown meeting of several hundred indignant citizens, a petition of 1,350 signatures demanded that Sheriff J. H. Boone take action.

Specifically, the reformers wanted Boone to arrest the prostitutes and abolish the zone. They insisted that saloons and gamblers obey the Sunday blue laws.

Boone growled that if El Pasoans wanted him to reform the gamblers and shady ladies, then he "was going to reform the reformers too."

The town essentially shut down on November 19, 1904. Sheriff Boone not only closed the tenderloin, but he also closed all candy shops, cigar stores, ice cream parlors and grocery stores. He charged them with violating the blue laws. He nearly closed the smelter (ASARCO) by arresting employees working on Sunday, and he even attempted to halt the streetcars.

It seemed all over for the reservation. Gamblers, ladies of easy virtue, and crowds of boozy sentimentalists went from house to house to say good-bye. When Sunday morning arrived, nearly five thousand people had crossed the river into Mexico. Signs nailed to brothel doors read, "We are spending our money in Juarez."

In 1910 C.E. "Henry" Kelly, a druggist, became mayor. Kelly blasted out Scenic Drive, installed sewers, improved the fire department and encouraged the creation of Texas State School of Mines and Metallurgy (now UT El Paso). He refused to restrain vice, and despised the reformers. That set the scene for the mayoral battle of the century between himself and Tom Lea, a slender, gun-toting, rising young lawyer as eloquent as he was fearless. Lea won by less than a thousand votes, and his first order instructed the police chief to stop collecting prostitution fines, saying his administration would not be supported with "the blood money of those unfortunate women." Furthermore, he planned to move the tenderloin to a more remote section of the city.

When all was said and done, however, it was the Texas Supreme Court that changed the morals of El Paso. It stunned everybody on December 8, 1915, by abolishing segregated vice. The reservation was illegal by Texas law, and since this meant the girls could no longer be confined to a particular district, they would likely spread into all sections of the community. Lea had no choice except to obey the commandment, and in January, 1916 he closed the zone of tolerance, although unofficially acknowledging that if the prostitutes settled south of Eighth Street, they would neither be molested nor subjected to fines.

Such an offer might have been a partial solution had it not been for military indignation. Fort Bliss rejected even an unofficial zone of prostitution, and threatened to place all El Paso off limits unless the tenderloin was totally banished. The mayor and council complied, and the Post, which up until this time had complained about vice only in downtown El Paso, was now surrounded with unsupervised and unregulated shady ladies. Lynchville sprang up near Fort Boulevard and Dyer, and became notorious for its sexual services.

Prostitution moved into roadhouses, motels, hotels, apartments and private homes. It wasn't until 1937 that El Paso finally mustered both the desire and the police enforcement to eradicate the practice almost completely.

The shift away from legalized prostitution was the most wrenching and controversial turning point in El Paso's four-hundred-year history. The practice prevailed for a half-century, and although the city took a giant stride toward respectability with its demise, the removal sacrificed much of El Paso's color, character and identification. The town would never again be the same.

Madams would no longer lustily shout, "Company in the parlor, girls." El Paso was a changed community without their presence. While the town may have done little more than export its prostitution to Juarez, it at least fumbled its way through a divisive period in the city's turbulent past.

One of the earliest pictures taken of Fort Bliss at its present location. This shows the first fourteen officers quarters as they looked in 1892–1893 along today's Sheridan Road. The buildings were yet to be occupied at the time this photograph was taken. The three structures at far right were noncommissioned officers quarters. The officers quarters are still occupied. [M.G. McKinney Collection]

11

When Fort Bliss Almost Moved to New Mexico

*Fort Bliss, the multi-million dollar installation
which for the past eighty years has been an
economic, social and community entity of El
Paso, might never have existed but for the
foresight of a few senior Army officers and the
persistent, concerted efforts of a small group of
energetic El Pasoans.*

George Ruhlen:
"The Genesis of New Fort Bliss," *Password*

El Paso almost lost Fort Bliss during the early 1890s when Washington considered abolishing it and establishing a large, regional post at Fort Selden, New Mexico, roughly ten miles north of Las Cruces.

For budget reasons, the government had previously closed Fort Bliss in January, 1877, a matter of poor timing because the El Paso Salt War promptly engulfed the county. A congressional investigation led to the Army's return on New Year's Day, 1878. Buffalo Soldiers of the 9th Cavalry and Company C of the 15th Infantry reoccupied old Camp Concordia, across I-10 from present-day Concordia Cemetery. After futile attempts to restore the adobe ruins, the troops leased quarters in downtown El Paso, and drilled on El Paso Street and in the Public Square (now San Jacinto Plaza). Soldiers called the community "Garrison Town."

A board of officers sought a permanent home, examining several locations in 1879 before recommending 135 acres alongside Hart's Mill in the present Hacienda Cafe area. Military labor constructed a post of masonry, adobe and wood. Officers quarters and barracks had porches; the roofs, shingles. A hospital treated a wide variety of ailments including venereal diseases, accidental and deliberate wounds, and intestinal disorders.

Boredom, demands of the flesh and the infrequency of regular pay undermined morale. Desertions climbed. Gambling and drinking flourished. "The moon was nearly full last night," wrote an *El Paso Times* reporter, but not "quite as full as some of the boys from Fort Bliss."

In 1881 the Santa Fe Railroad split the parade ground with tracks, while the Southern Pacific skirted the post's eastern perimeter. Both lines disrupted life and duties, and made intoxication especially hazardous when trains were moving. However, the tracks brought benefits too. Supplies could be conveniently loaded and unloaded, and troops rapidly shipped to practically any region of the country.

Fort Bliss was a way station to the Arizona Indian Wars. Generals George Crook and Nelson Miles visited. Lieutenant Britton Davis and his chief of scouts, Al Sieber, brought sixteen Apache scouts to the fort where they rested prior to leaving for the pursuit of Geronimo. The scouts tracked him across the treacherous heights of Sonora's Sierra Madres, causing his eventual surrender. The Army then forced Geronimo and his followers to board the Southern Pacific and go into Florida exile. Even the Apache scouts, no longer useful, went into exile on the same train. As the Southern Pacific chugged through Fort Bliss on its forlorn way east, Geronimo described the military buildings as "chicken coops."

But as the 1880s closed and Indian wars became fanciful memories of old soldiers, the Army owned dozens of small, temporary, bug-infested, isolated, unhealthy posts. Authorities considered them too expensive to maintain and too detrimental to efficiency. Where once these forts had denied rest to the red man, they were now relics of a bygone era.

Railroads had changed the nature of warfare. They could transport an enemy to where he could run no more — as Geronimo would have testified. They could make the military so mobile that the Indian virtually lost the advantages of remote terrain. Soldiers could quickly reach any Indian country by railroad, and in the process be more rested, better supplied, and more easily reinforced.

Brevet Major General John Pope wrote Secretary of War Robert T. Lincoln that "the large military interest will be best served by the establishment of one large post to replace several smaller ones." Lincoln believed Selden could replace forts Craig, Cummings, McRae and Thorn in New Mexico and Bowie and Grant in Arizona. Bliss was not mentioned, but Lieutenant General Phil Sheridan had it in mind, commenting that "for the protection of . . . El Paso I deem it best to concentrate not far from there a considerable number of troops." Even General William T. Sherman concurred, writing Secretary Lincoln that a permanent post should be built at Selden. The Government could abolish all "the little adobe and *jacal* forts now held for a radius of 250 miles."

Gradually the word got out. Fort Bliss would give way to Fort Selden. Selden had been named for Colonel Henry Raymond Selden, a Vermonter who fought in the Mexican War, the Seminole uprisings, the Indian wars, and through several Civil War engagements in New Mexico. He died in 1865 while in command of Fort Union, and four months later Fort Selden was established in his honor at the southern extremity of the *Jornada del Muerto,* the Dead Man's Route, the bloody and dreaded Spanish highway where the road left the Rio Grande a short distance north of Las Cruces.

Captain Arthur MacArthur commanded Fort Selden from 1884 to 1886. His son Douglas—who won fame during World War II and Korea— encountered a camel wandering loose in the nearby desert, a remnant of the 1855 camel experiment by the Army.

The military anticipated that Fort Selden troops could invade Chihuahua if trouble occurred. Selden had plenty of land and water. It could move against restless Indians, and it would quickly react along the border. And it would soon have access to a railroad connecting Denver with El Paso.

Fort Bliss had several serious disadvantages because of its location. The water was unhealthy. The trains were disruptive. A nearby smelter (ASARCO) emitted "poisonous" fumes. There was no room for expansion, no space for large depots and warehouses. Its position in a bowl surrounded by mountains made it vulnerable to artillery placed on the heights.

But fortunately for El Paso, the decision about Selden was never anything but talk. Bickering army officers and a siesta-inclined Congress rarely conferred. No substantial sums of money were appropriated, no construction started. No citizens insisted that the military and the government meet their obligations.

Meanwhile, General Sherman visited Fort Bliss and decided to support it. He agreed the fort was small, but suggested that infantry be stationed there and cavalry at Fort Cummings, near Deming, New Mexico. Sherman needed civilian assistance for his views to prevail, so in 1887 the El Paso Development Board (Chamber of Commerce) published a pamphlet, *El Paso As A Military Post*. With maps, charts, statistics and plenty of weighty words, it described El Paso's ten thousand people as having property valued at $5 million. It spoke of 150 businesses, three banks, two smelters, six churches, two stockyards and four public schools. It even had an $80,000 opera house.

Nevertheless, Fort Selden still held the high ground in Washington, thanks largely to the unceasing efforts of General Benjamin Grierson, commander of the District of New Mexico. Along with the Santa Fe Ring, which controlled New Mexico politics, he repeatedly overstepped his jurisdiction and demanded the abolishment of Fort Bliss. More than any other military figure, Grierson kept Fort Selden constantly in contention as the regional selection, and it wasn't until 1890 that the issue conclusively went El Paso's way. Congress authorized $150,000 to purchase between 300 and 640 acres within ten miles of El Paso. However, when the bill cleared both houses, it had been changed. The money could be spent only for construction; it would not purchase land. Furthermore, the government insisted upon one thousand acres, all of it donated. Officials in Washington had read *El Paso As A Military Post,* had noted the signatures, and observed where El Pasoans had promised to furnish land for Fort Bliss if necessary.

El Paso hesitated, uncertain of whether to proceed. The cost would be over $9,000, prompting *The El Paso Times* to blast local indifference and lethargy. It said one thousand troops would put $14,000 into the local economy each month. It dwelled on "fat government contracts," and stressed the consequences should the funds not be raised. "Laredo and Deming would like to get a chance at (Fort Bliss) for 24 hours, while San Antonio does not believe we *have* nine thousand dollars."

Finally, the El Paso Progressive Association asked the Army to select a site so that the land might be purchased. In mid-July, a military board settled on one thousand acres northeast of the city, precisely where the headquarters complex of Fort Bliss exists today. Much of this property lay along the proposed White Oaks Railroad and belonged to Charles R. Morehead, president of the State National Bank. He would get $20 an acre for 176 acres owned by himself and B. H. Davis. The rest of the land sold for $6.25 and $5.00 an acre. In all, one hundred of El Paso's most prosperous individuals subscribed $9,235 for the thousand acres. The money also paid for a well to insure sufficient water. Morehead and Davis kicked in $1,000 each.

But the government wasn't satisfied. It needed boundaries to discourage undesirable saloons and brothels, and it requested a donation of additional acres along the mesa's edge near the proposed railroad tracks to about where Dyer Street is now. Today this mesa section is called Officers Row. The land also provided the best trace for a wagon road, today's Pershing entrance. Captain George Ruhlen, in charge of construction at Fort Bliss, had the unhappy task of explaining this extra need to the citizens. The news stunned the Progressive Committee, and before it could recover, the Army demanded even more. In a take-it-or-leave-it ultimatum, the Army insisted upon 266 acres in addition to the original 1,000. The figure gave citizens cardiac arrest, and furious letters punctuated the negotiations. The Progressive Committee argued that it had complied with the law, acquiesced with the site selection, raised the funds for purchase, sunk a well to establish suitable water, and finally turned over a land title to the federal government.

Still, El Paso could either raise another $6,825, or forget about an army post. The second subscription drive was not easy, but forty people reluctantly provided the money. The Army was now pleased.

For its part, the government increased its Fort Bliss investment to $300,000, and construction started in 1892. This would not be a post created with troop labor. For months the headquarters complex resembled a small city as civilian workers built modern buildings. The structures had plumbing, brick, sewage, pure water, trees, grass, coal to burn instead of mesquite roots. A marvel of the age made newspaper headlines when a telegraph line hooked the city to the fort.

There were no cost overruns. Congress appropriated $300,000, and $136.56 was returned to the treasury.

And the Army generously made concessions to El Paso. The old post cemetery, at what is now Cleveland Square and the Library block, was presented to the city. President Cleveland signed the release, and had the park named in his honor.

Fort Bliss on the mesa, the sixth and final location, opened in 1893, but not as the huge regimental post so often promised by the Army and so often anticipated by the citizens of El Paso. The fort languished for approximately ten years, and only the Mexican Revolution of 1910 raised it to the largest cavalry post in the nation.

Fort Selden was abandoned, and is today a New Mexico historical site. Through a series of struggles followed by stubborn perseverance, Fort Bliss remained at El Paso, by far the best bargain in local history. El Paso simply cannot be imagined without it. The two are not only neighbors; they are friends.

El Pasoans and Mexican revolutionaries line the Rio Grande in 1911 at a point near present-day ASARCO. Guns, food, money, ammunition, clothing and tall (and true) tales swapped sides. It was a time unique in American history. [El Paso Public Library]

12

The Battle of Juarez

It was a long time coming, but that only
prolonged the poignancy of the delight of it, for
I maintain that never was there such a colorful,
romantic, noble and foolish period as the first
revolution in northern Mexico. Juarez and El
Paso formed the center of it.
Timothy G. Turner:
Bullets, Bottles and Gardenias

Timothy G. Turner was a young reporter for the *El Paso Herald* when the Mexican Revolution started in 1911 at Ciudad Juarez, Chihuahua. His book, *Bullets, Bottles and Gardenias,* is the finest firsthand account to emerge, and the world owes much to Turner's journalistic zeal. He gave the Revolution life, color and zest, introducing characters who might today be unknown were it not for him. But most of all, Timothy Turner provided romance and simplicity to a struggle now known as brutish and complex.

The central figures read like characters in a Russian novel: Porfirio Díaz, the President of Mexico; William Howard Taft, the President of the United States; Francisco Madero, revolutionary leader and future Mexican President; Ricardo Flores Magón, anarchist and philosopher; Pascual Orozco and Francisco "Pancho" Villa, guerrilla leaders of murderous but creative ability.

The excesses and ambitions of Porfirio Díaz brought on the Revolution. The ailing dictator had been a national hero during the French invasion of the early 1860s. Ten years afterwards he overthrew Mexican President Lerdo de Tejada, implementing policies to encourage railroads, agriculture, banking and industry. Mexico slowly emerged from its own Dark Ages, but in the process Díaz sold the country's birthright to foreigners, especially the English, Germans and Americans.

Of perhaps greater significance, Díaz did not know when to quit. His thirty year rule permitted no criticism, no political parties, and no heirs apparent. The President believed these measures would not only insure his longevity in office, but would bring national stability. Instead they made revolution inevitable.

Díaz sought self-preservation by strengthening ties with the United States. Díaz and American President Taft met at El Paso and Juarez in 1909. The Porfiriato wanted credibility. Taft wanted to buttress his "Dollar Diplomacy," a derisive term for American financial interests in Mexico.

"I am not quite sure at whose insistence this meeting was held," Taft wrote his wife, "but I do know that I received a communication, perhaps directly from the old man, of an informal character, saying how glad he would be to have such a meeting brought about. He thinks, and I believe rightly, that the knowledge throughout his country of the friendship of the United States will strengthen him with his own people, and tend to discourage revolutionary efforts to establish a different government."

The conference in October 1909 accomplished little. Presidents shuffled back and forth across the international line and made lofty pronouncements of inconsequential substance. In his only speech, Taft intoned, "The prosperity of the United States is largely dependent upon the prosperity of Mexico, and Mexico's prosperity upon ours." Then he visited the El Paso Chamber of Commerce, plopped his ponderous bulk into a chair, and cracked its leg.

Díaz considered the meeting a triumph. A ninety minute parade through downtown El Paso brought modest cheers. The solemn Díaz, in the full dress of a Division General, with a multiplicity of glistening medals, bowed to the crowds. For his remaining fifteen months as president, this would be his finest hour.

The conference failed to slacken any revolutionary fervor among Mexican intellectuals. Ricardo Flores Magón in particular had enough real and imagined grievances to warrant psychotherapy for a dozen unhappy zealots. With his brothers he launched the Revolution's most radical and influential newspaper, *Regeneración,* an El Paso publication appealing primarily to the tiny intellectual group with influence in the industrial and mining occupations where concentrated workers lived in misery.

Nor was Ricardo a simple man with an ordinary, uncomplicated philosophy. His harangues excited the literate class, but his mania for finding enemies, both Mexican and American, behind every establishment bush led him into unwise and damaging associations. Harassment and prison failed to quench his fiery ardor, and across the years he shifted from a classic liberal to an anarchist. Since he did not recognize ruling bodies, he did not acknowledge laws either. His relationship with bomb throwers made it easy to track his whereabouts, and it furnished American authorities with a multitude of excuses to arrest him. Ricardo Flores Magón would die in Leavenworth Prison.

The mantle of leadership therefore needed a more practical commander, and it is ironic that it fell to a moderate who never considered himself a revolutionary.

The gentle Francisco Madero wanted change, not ruin. He came from a large and wealthy Coahuila family, professed admiration for the American political system, and believed Mexico could be governed by democratic means. Madero wanted the nation back on the constitutional track with one term per president. This radiant do-gooder, filled with honesty and charity, a tiny man with a birdlike voice, somehow began uniting the brawling factions, particularly in the northern Mexican states with their disgruntled, pistol-toting desert dwellers.

For a while it seemed that a revolution might be avoided. Díaz implied he would retire, and Madero announced for President in 1910. Then Díaz changed his mind, resenting a popular opponent as a reminder of slipping prestige. The police jailed Madero in San Luis Potosí, holding him until Díaz counted the votes. Then with the mellowing President assured of victory, Madero "escaped."

Madero fled across the border at Laredo, and plotted an uprising in Puebla. Díaz crushed it easily and executed its leaders. Undeterred, Madero tried a similar attempt in the border town of Ciudad Porfirio Diaz (modern Piedras Negras). After waiting across the Rio Grande in Texas for shots that never roared, Madero prudently cancelled an uprising that never started.

The despairing Madero now made the most brilliant decision of his "military" career. He could carry the Revolution to El Paso and Juarez.

Compared to a million-plus people living today in the El Paso-Ciudad Juarez complex, Juarez in 1910 had nearly eleven thousand people and

El Paso almost forty thousand. The region was (and still is) the largest port of entry into and out of Mexico. El Paso had five rail networks. Across the Rio Grande, the Mexican Central Railroad extended from Mexico City to Juarez, the only line connecting both the capital and the border. Across those rails fanned the majority of land trade between the two nations, and it took no military genius to see that a Juarez under revolutionary control could choke the Mexican economy. Furthermore, whoever controlled customs also had access to a large percentage of foreign exchange—enough money to equip an army.

Over in El Paso, fifty percent of the population was Hispanic, and almost all despised the Díaz regime. Anglos supported the revolutionists. *The El Paso Times* and the *El Paso Herald* showed revolutionary bents.

The town had long been a refuge for Mexican political exiles, and their Spanish language newspapers flourished in South El Paso. Titles proliferated like *Revista Ilustrada, Diario de El Paso, El Clarín del Norte* and *El Echo del Comercio. La Reforma,* an 8 by 11 inch sheet printed on one side, stated proudly that "We fight for the dignity of high and moral principles. We seek the rational truth, the moral law, and finally, progress and goodness."

These newspapers generally resembled handbills, and were published on a now-and-then basis when finances permitted. Few offered any practical solutions to Mexico's agony. The editors considered compromise and moderation to be treason. Their fuzzy goals sounded impressive only to other social-anarchists. Editorials had emotional, oftentimes hysterical overtones, and editors frequently denounced the United States (which protected their right to publish) as savagely as they criticized Díaz and each other.

Guerrilla fighters were generally spared the ambiguous meanderings of journalistic prose. But those gutty men with rusted and multi-caliber rifles knew how to fight. Upon their ragged but proud backs rode the only practical hopes of the Mexican insurgency.

It is a wonder that somehow these untutored warriors came to love an eccentric such as Francisco Madero. Like most mystics, Madero could be arrogant as well as unfathomable. He was a spiritualist and a vegetarian. His high-pitched voice quavered, and he found it difficult to impress or influence macho Mexicans when he had to stand on a stool to see their faces.

But he possessed an uncompromising if oftentimes nebulous appeal that touched the hearts of young and old, rich and poor, sophisticated

Mexican revolutionaries charge into the Battle of Juarez, 1911.
[El Paso Public Library]

and humble. Madero spoke for Mexico, and even after listening to him speak, and then wondering what he said, people still correctly perceived that here was a man dedicated to a more promising homeland. Madero's squeaky exhortations found receptive listeners all along the border, and especially at the Pass of the North. For El Paso made possible the success of the Mexican Revolution. El Paso furnished some manpower, plus lots of supplies, refuge and moral support. El Paso was the jumping-off point for the Mexican Revolution, and it was all done with state, local and federal governments looking the other way.

In the meantime, war correspondents flocked to the Pass, an assortment of odd-balls and brilliant journalists. John Kenneth Turner, author of *Barbarous Mexico,* arrived with Gutiérrez de Lara, full time socialist and part time newspaperman. Lara wept during battles.

Felix A. Sommerfeld, a barrel-chested, enigmatic German, passed himself off as a reporter for the United Press. Yet he was also an intelligence officer for gun-runners, and a business agent for Francisco Madero and Pancho Villa.

Correspondents clustered in the Orndorff (now Cortez) and Sheldon (now Plaza) hotels, congregating in off hours at "Bill Reid's Place" in the cellar beneath the City National Bank. L. N. Spears and Stephen Bonsal represented the *New York Times.* The *New York Herald* sent Earl

Harding, who worried so about premature baldness that he shaved his head and hoped the hair would grow bushier. Otheman Stevens of the *Los Angeles Examiner,* took only a drop or two of liquor in his high-balls, and became an object of scorn among correspondents.

Rodney Gilbert, a Philadelphia newspaperman, wore a straw hat until he acquired lice. Alfred Henry Lewis, a magazine and book writer, refused to sit unless he had a stool, and war correspondent James Hare tried repeatedly to photograph the stiff and formal General Juan Navarro, commander of the Federal garrison in Juarez.

Gerald Brandon and Leopoldo Zea came up from Mexico City for *El Diario.* They were joined by Luis Malvais of *El País* and Ramírez de Aguilar of *Imparcial.* The *El Paso Times* and the *El Paso Herald* kept correspondents in the field.

The press needed news to justify its existence, and the reporters found plenty to discuss in Pascual Orozco and Doroteo Arango (who would became world famous as Pancho Villa).

The moody Orozco and the flamboyant Villa had a talent for winning battles and an ability to make correct decisions from the saddle. But the revolutionaries would never be anything but brigands until they rallied around a national leader. They were insurgents seeking respectability while, over in El Paso, the respectable Madero sought an effective army.

In early 1911, Orozco captured a Kansas City, Mexico and Orient train and spread a rumor that he planned to invade Chihuahua City. As Federals guarded the state capital, Orozco marched north and vowed to attack Juarez on February 5, if Madero would assume command. Villa joined him, and nine days later so did Madero.

Juarez took on the appearance of a ghost town. General Navarro cursed the bitter cold, and wondered how long his poorly equipped army could survive. Even reinforcements were a mixed blessing. Two hundred men arrived without ammunition, with half their wives and camp followers barefoot and frostbitten, several in advanced stages of pregnancy.

Juarez males feared impressment into both armies, so they and their families fled to El Paso. Mexican businesses closed. The Banco Minero, the Banco Nacional, and the post office transferred assets to El Paso.

Francisco Madero established his headquarters across the Rio Grande from the smelter (today's ASARCO), in a windowless, one-room adobe hut with a dirt floor. His army contained teenage boys with giant grins, their Mausers dragging the ground. Old men with white beards carried guns that operated only with effort, while lithe Yaqui warriors tested their bows and tried to keep their long raven hair from their eyes. This odd assortment of humanity shared one common identity: a steadfast belief that they were the best damn fighters in the world.

Soldiers of fortune reinforced the restless revolutionaries. The tall, austere General Benjamin Johannes Viljoen of Boer War fame strapped on his field glasses and sold his services to Madero. Giuseppe Garibaldi, grandson of ''Red Shirt'' Garibaldi, the military hero who united Italy, joined the rebels. Between thirty and fifty Americans enlisted, all of them reluctant to reveal identities.

American recruits formed squads called ''foreign legions'' by the newspapers. Garibaldi defined his supporters as ''groups,'' whereas Viljoen used ''commandos,'' a Boer term. The Mexicans considered everybody *gente,* meaning people or folk. They were the *gente de Orozco* or the *gente de Villa.*

A suspension bridge crossed the Rio Grande at the smelter, and hundreds of Americans walked and gawked among the revolutionaries. Money, guns, food and ammunition changed hands.

Abraham González, eventual governor of Chihuahua, talked El Paso physician Dr. Ira Bush into becoming chief surgeon for Madero. The stocky Bush, who looked like an Indian, would write *Gringo Doctor,* and open an *insurrecto* (insurgent) hospital at 410 South Campbell.

During April, envoys met for three weeks inside a clump of trees three hundred yards west of the present Hacienda Cafe in El Paso. The site became ''Peace Grove.'' When talks ended in stalemate, Madero lost his confidence and refused to order an assault. He suspected that Navarro had grown too strong, and he feared United States intervention if stray shots killed any El Pasoans. Instead, Madero moved south, saying it would be better strategy to attack Casas Grandes.

His reluctance to strike Juarez astonished Orozco and Villa, so they ordered an immediate assault. Foreign Legions led the way on May 8, 1911.

Rebel squads of fifteen to twenty men trotted through the dry *acequia madre* (main irrigation ditch) into the heart of Juarez, dynamiting a house holding nearly forty Federals and shooting them as they fled. The insurgents took the Mexican Central Railroad bridge and the Stanton Street bridge. They captured the Ketelsen & Degetau warehouse and overran the bullring, Our Lady of Guadalupe Mission and the post office building.

Over in El Paso, thousands of men, women and children lined the river banks and watched from rooftops. At least a dozen died or were

Juarez military headquarters of Federal General Juan Navarro. Navarro escaped into El Paso, but holes in the adobe wall bear a tragic, eloquent witness to the fate of less fortunate comrades. The bloodstained plaster is a testimonial of how brave men made the ultimate sacrifice for supporting the Díaz regime. [Cochise County Historical Society-Arizona]

wounded by stray bullets. From his position on top of the El Paso Laundry, Judge Joseph Sweeney described the scene at night. "It was a beautiful sight to see the shrapnel bursting up in the air and scattering its death-dealing missiles in the hills and valleys surrounding," he wrote.

After three days of fighting, rebels cleared the central plaza and captured the Federal barracks. Tired, thirsty and demoralized, Navarro hung out the white flag at one o'clock in the afternoon. Garibaldi accepted the surrender.

An unreal scene greeted El Pasoans when they swarmed across the border. As firing squads settled old scores, the camera never focused on a single act of cowardice. The doomed stood stoically, ignoring the bodies of executed comrades and calmly awaited the awful rifles.

Dr. John W. Cathcart operated a portable X-ray and treated wounded men carried into the smelter hospital. He and his daughter, Florence (Melby), then entered Juarez, and the memory of *insurrectos* and soldiers maimed by dynamite and artillery rounds, their arms and legs amputated and scattered in the streets, remain forever etched in her memory.

Orozco and Villa wanted General Navarro added to the dead, but Madero, who had returned to take charge, refused to permit the execution. Smugglers sneaked Navarro across the Rio Grande and into the Popular Dry Goods where he hid in the chinaware department for three days before slipping into Hotel Dieu Hospital.

The city's capture disheartened President Porfirio Díaz. He could either resign, or plunge his country deeper into chaos. To his credit he entered exile. On the night of May 21, representatives from both factions signed the "Treaty of Ciudad Juarez" in the glare of automobile headlights outside the Customs House.

The first battle of Juarez had ended. Madero became President but was soon assassinated by one of his own generals. For the next twenty years, Mexico writhed in continued warfare as Pancho Villa, Victoriano Huerta, Emiliano Zapata, Álvaro Obregón and Venustiano Carranza sank the country repeatedly in a welter of misery. Ciudad Juarez became the most fought-over city on the North American continent, changing hands six times during the Mexican Revolution (1911-1930).

And in the process, the Revolution proved a significant turning point for El Paso.

The town reaped enormous national and international newspaper coverage. General John J. "Black Jack" Pershing took command at Fort Bliss in 1914 and turned it into America's largest cavalry post. (Fort Bliss had previously been infantry.) More soldiers were stationed at Fort Bliss than anywhere since the Civil War. National guardsmen lined the river and guarded the bridges. The military payroll galvanized a massive economic development. When the Punitive Expedition began in 1916 (after Pancho Villa's raid on Columbus, New Mexico), El Paso supplied an army in Chihuahua.

Thousands of Mexican refugees enriched the Pass with their culture. Many were doctors, lawyers and professional persons. Whereas hundreds eventually returned to Mexico, the majority remained and left their unique mark upon the city. Excluding recent immigration, perhaps eighty percent of all Hispanics residing in the United States today owe their roots in this country not to the early conquistadors but to parents and grandparents who fled the fire and blood of Pancho Villa.

The Battle of Juarez, 1911, changed El Paso from just a railroad stop to a city conscious of its history and concerned about its destiny. Some of this realization stemmed from publicity, part from economic stimulation, and part from different ideas and views of the world as brought in by outsiders. The citizens of El Paso for the first time ever started to think of themselves as mainstream Texans and Americans, an intrepid people who had participated in a cause greater than themselves.

Elephant Butte Dam under construction circa 1915. The butte itself is at the upper right. Some water is being released to keep the moisture level below the construction work in progress. [Frank Mangan Collection]

13

The Elephant Butte Saga

When the Mexican minister, Matías Romero,
heard about the [Elephant Butte] dam he
vigorously protested it; he wanted a dam nearer
the border. If the Elephant Butte reservoir were
built, there would not be any water for a lower
one [at El Paso], resulting inevitably, he
believed, in the abandonment of the Juarez
Valley.

Norris Hundley, Jr.: *Dividing the Waters*

Nearly a hundred years ago, the concept of Elephant Butte Dam shook the governments in Washington and Mexico City. It created a rift between El Paso and New Mexico, and started the water controversy of the century.

When finally built, Elephant Butte Dam dramatically improved the economic strength of El Paso and Juarez. But what happened prior to construction was a classic tale of hocus-pocus and idealism struggling toward both mutual and divergent ends.

The tale begins with a Rio Grande that was essentially two streams. The upper portion originated on the eastern slopes of the Continental Divide in southwestern Colorado. After slicing through New Mexico, the river flowed past El Paso and dwindled practically to puddle status prior to the Big Bend. The Rio Conchos, with its headwaters in Mexico, fed the lower portion of the Rio Grande. It entered the channel at Presidio and continued to the sea.

During the 1880s, Mexico complained that Colorado and New Mexico were consuming the Rio Grande before it reached the international border at Juarez. Mexico justified a prior right to the water because of ancient usage, a rationale recognized by international law.

Texas supported the Mexican claim because if Juarez had no access to the Rio Grande's water, neither would El Paso. Furthermore, since the Rio Conchos supplied the lower Rio Grande, Texas wanted the United States to be generous with the upper river so that Mexico might be equally magnanimous with the lower.

Washington wavered, recognizing an approaching litigious nightmare if a settlement with Mexico wasn't forthcoming. Since the government needed expert advice, it turned to John Wesley Powell, the brilliant, eccentric, one-armed champion for conservation in the American West. Powell arranged a military transfer to El Paso for Major Anson Mills, a man already familiar with the Pass, a diplomat skilled in engineering.

The caustic, irascible Mills had laid out the street system in 1859 and named it El Paso. He rose to captain during the Civil War and to major during the subsequent Indian wars. The Army transferred him to Fort Selden, New Mexico (ten miles north of Las Cruces), to investigate water troubles, and from there assigned him to Fort Bliss. In 1894 the Army retired Mills as a brigadier general, and the government appointed him as the American boundary commissioner.

Mills believed plenty of water still flowed in the channel, it just flowed at the wrong time. In 1888, he electrified the American Southwest and northern Mexico by calling for an international dam at El Paso. It would store the water until needed by farmers.

Congress approved the idea in April, 1890, but neglected to appropriate funds. Four years later an exasperated Mexico sued the United States for $35 million.

The Department of State sought additional information about the alleged water shortage at Juarez, so in 1896 Mills assigned his reliable assistant W. W. Follett to survey the upper Rio Grande. Follett concluded that dying fruit trees, abandoned fields and dry canals had led to a population decline in Juarez. Mexico had "been wrongfully deprived for many years of . . . a portion of her equitable rights to . . . one-half of the Rio Grande," Follett wrote.

Mills and Mexican Boundary Commissioner Francisco Javier Osorno drafted a proposed treaty calling for an equal distribution of Rio Grande water and for the construction of an international dam at El Paso.

The Americans would absorb all costs, and the reservoir would be built about one mile north of the El Paso smelter (present-day ASARCO).

Washington might have confirmed the agreement had not an "embarrassment" arisen. Without notifying the State Department, the secretary of interior had already licensed a private firm to build a dam near Engle, New Mexico, a remote site 120 miles north of El Paso and near a point called Elephant Butte.

A furious Mills accused several El Pasoans of conspiring against regional best interests. He denounced City Engineer John L. Campbell, realtor Albert M. Loomis, and casket salesman Edward V. Berrien, saying they advocated the New Mexico dam. With the First National Bank, and the law firm of Davis, Beall and Kemp, they formed the "Rio Grande Dam and Irrigation Company," installing as director the fiery Nathan Ellington Boyd, a Virginia physician living in Mesilla, New Mexico.

When the capital fell short, Boyd recruited a British company with experience in the Nile Valley. The firm committed itself to the largest artificial lake in the world at Engle. It would recover its investment through property sales and water rights. Farmers would cede one-half of their land to the corporation in return for water rights to the other half. They would still pay an annual fee of $1.50 per acre irrigated. The British anticipated a $15 million profit each year.

Mexico would receive no allotment. If Washington wanted Mexico to have free water, then the United States should "subsidize the company $250,000 a year."

Should the Engle project prevail, El Paso would lose its dam. Mills complained to the secretary of state, who defined the Rio Grande as a navigable stream, a piece of legal fiction purposely inserted in the Treaty of Guadalupe Hidalgo. If Elephant Butte curtailed Rio Grande navigation, then the dam was illegal.

Anson Mills agreed to document the river's navigability. Mills mentioned flatboats plying the river north of Juarez. He described logs floating downstream. Army engineers Captain George McDerby and Major A. M. Miller swore the Rio Grande would float ships near El Paso during specific seasons.

In May 1897 acting Attorney General Holmes Conrad filed an injunction in Albuquerque against the British company, insisting that a dam at Engle would paralyze Rio Grande navigation.

The syndicate somehow failed to realize its economic peril, believing the dispute was a misunderstanding. "It must not be supposed that the United States government is antagonistic to the company," Boyd wrote. "To the contrary, we have reason to believe the United States government is the reverse of unfriendly."

While Boyd patiently waited for Washington to regain its senses, Mills launched a river survey to determine navigability between San Marcial, New Mexico (fifty miles north of Engle), and Laredo, Texas. Boundary engineers in 1901 suffered from quicksand, dry channels, floods, mosquitoes and monotony. A rattlesnake bit consulting engineer P. D. Cunningham on the toe as he slept near Langtry, Texas and he spent a week recovering. A week later when twenty-five miles from Eagle Pass, Cunningham's skiff struck a submerged boulder and he drowned.

The navigability report bolstered the government's case, proving to Mills' satisfaction that the Rio Grande could support steamers. The English dam would obviously destroy this navigation, although Mills never said, and nobody ever asked, why a dam at El Paso would not do the same.

Boyd furiously responded. He hurled twelve charges at Mills, including perjury, treason, fraud and conspiracy. Boyd accused Secretary of State John Hay of "having a long and full knowledge of the facts." Boyd vowed to bring this "official crime" to the attention of the President, and said, "I will horsewhip Secretary Hay in some public place and thereby secure my own arrest and the necessary publicity." He correctly perceived a government conspiracy of silence, and said, "It should not be necessary for me [Boyd] to sacrifice myself further by publicly pulling John Hay's nose, or caning him, or putting a bullet through him, in order to arouse sufficient public interest in my charges to insure their proper investigation."

Three times the case went to trial in New Mexico. Three times Boyd won. But three times the United States Supreme Court overruled the decision and sent it back to lower court.

On May 23, 1903, it all dramatically ended. Washington cancelled the Engle contract because the firm had failed to build a dam within five years as required by law. Of course, the company could hardly fulfill its obligation since the United States kept it in court most of that time.

The British company filed a breach of contract suit, lost and went bankrupt. Colonel W. J. Engledue, designer for the Imperial Irrigation Works in India and a consultant for the dam, committed suicide. Boyd accused Mills of causing Engledue's death and P. D. Cunningham's as well.

Boyd spent the rest of his life a bitter man. Anson Mills went on to argue a boundary dispute known as the Chamizal, an international disagreement as to whether the Rio Grande at El Paso had been moving south into Juarez at a rapid or gradual rate. When the dispute went to arbitration and the United States lost, Mills refused to accept the decision. The Chamizal festered until the 1960s when enlightened statesmanship resolved the controversy. In the meantime, the State Department forced Mills out as the American boundary commissioner.

The way was now open for a dam at the Pass, and Congress created the Bureau of Reclamation in 1902. It listened to a litany of angry New Mexico complaints that an El Paso dam would deny the Territory water. It especially upset residents that a dam at El Paso would drown much of the fertile Mesilla Valley in New Mexico.

Time and legalities stopped El Paso. A survey of bedrock in the Pass revealed serious structural weaknesses. Furthermore, since Texas had no public lands, El Paso could not qualify for reclamation funds. The issue languished until November 1904 when the National Irrigation Congress met in El Paso. A week later El Paso relinquished its claim for a dam because of government assurances that the community would receive irrigation water stored with reclamation funds.

Elephant Butte Dam became a reality, and its reservoir covered Engle. After numerous delays, construction started in 1912 and finished in 1916. Three diversion dams—Leasburg, Mesilla and Percha—channeled water into New Mexico's irrigation ditches.

To generate electricity, however, water had to be released through the dam, even when it wasn't needed for irrigation. As authorities pondered the loss, studies showed that fifty percent of all drainage from thunderstorms between Elephant Butte and El Paso actually accumulated within thirty miles downstream of the Butte. The obvious solution called for a catch basin there, a reservoir today called Caballo Dam.

Meanwhile, Mexico and the United States had signed a treaty in 1906 for an equitable distribution of the upper Rio Grande. Mexico accepted sixty-thousand acre-feet of water at Juarez on an annual basis, a fraction of what ordinarily rolled down the channel. The El Paso valley gets whatever else reaches the Pass.

A dependable, regular supply of water transformed the El Paso and Juarez valleys into highly productive cotton farms. The Rio Grande Rectification Treaty and the Rio Grande Canalization Project during the 1930s and 1940s straightened the river from Elephant Butte to the eastern tip of the El Paso-Juarez valley, shortening the valley from 155 river miles to 86.

Counties along the river divided themselves into water districts, and by paying a fixed amount per acre, a farmer could irrigate his land. Today El Paso receives about thirteen percent of the river water for utility purposes. But back when Elephant Butte came on stream, El Paso could have assured itself of a steady supply sufficient for much of its future had it not been for a shortsighted city council denying the modest cost. The aldermen anticipated an inexhaustible reserve of pure, cheap water from the Hueco Bolson, a field between the Franklin and Hueco mountains.

Today, as the Hueco Bolson is slowly depleted, the city has delayed calamity by filing suit against New Mexico for a share of the Mesilla Bolson, a field north of El Paso.

Even these underground water holes will not last indefinitely, and it will eventually come down to El Paso either legally taking the irrigation water for municipal use or facing a municipal growth reduction. By law the Rio Grande is allocated only for irrigation. However, when the underground supplies vanish, El Paso will petition for the Elephant Butte releases, except for the Mexican guarantee, and farming will reluctantly yield to the greater need. Local agriculture and irrigation, like the struggle for the dam, will become just a memory, a subject for musings by future historians.

14

Restless River, Disputed Land

The United States said it was erosion; Mexico
said it was avulsion. The argument grew
more heated as the disputed Chamizal grew
more valuable. Probably more communications
have been exchanged and more arguments
presented over this square mile of land than any
piece of property of comparable size in the
world.

Conrey Bryson: *The Land Where We Live*

The Chamizal controversy and settlement decisively changed El Paso
and Juarez. It made the two cities better neighbors and friends; it modi-
fied their geographic and economic face; and it resolved an emotional,
turbulent, legal conflict.

For nearly one hundred years the Chamizal poisoned relations between
the United States and Mexico. Its essentials began in 1827 when wealthy
Juarez merchant and trader, Ponce de León, purchased 211 acres of mud
flats comprising the lower downtown section of present-day El Paso.
The unstable Rio Grande formed the southern and western boundary.
Following a marauding flood in 1830, Ponce nearly doubled his hold-
ings when the river bit strongly into the south bank and eroded portions
of Juarez.

Since Mexico owned both sides of the Rio Grande, the channel shifts
had only nuisance consequences. But those mellow times disappeared

in 1848 when the Mexican War ended. The Treaty of Guadalupe Hidalgo established the Rio Grande as the border between the United States and Mexico, and the two countries formed an international boundary commission. It surveyed the river during the early 1850s.

The Treaty had no provisions should the Rio Grande change its channel. The United States and Mexico later agreed that any *sudden* channel shift would not affect the boundary. It would stay in the *original* bed, no matter how dusty. However, if the channel *gradually* eroded, then the existing river remained as the boundary. The key was *speed* of change, and the diplomats failed to define how fast was fast and how slow was slow.

Shortly after the Mexican War, Ponce leased his rancho to Benjamin Franklin Coons, a trader and developer, who apparently failed to make payments. The land was repossessed and sold to William T. "Uncle Billy" Smith, a dreamer, mountain man, wagonmaster and itinerant developer. Smith sold the grant to the El Paso Company, developers who retained Anson Mills to survey a townsite. Mills finished in February 1859, and in the process gained an additional thirty-five acres because the river had continued its active erosion into Mexico.

By 1867, Matías Romero, the Mexican minister to Washington, complained that a Juarez district named for *chamiso* bushes (the Chamizal) had been disappearing into El Paso. The minister wanted American recognition of Mexican sovereignty in that region north of the international boundary.

Washington responded that the Rio Grande had indeed eroded Juarez, but defined the changes as "slow and gradual." It disallowed the claim, and El Paso incorporated the Chamizal into its Second Ward. However, when El Paso dumped raw sewage through a twelve inch pipe across the district and into the Rio Grande, Mexico protested the use of the Chamizal to undermine "the health of the towns lying opposite."

The State Department asked Texas to investigate, and Governor Lawrence Sullivan Ross again refused Mexican jurisdiction in Chamizal. Furthermore, he said the sewage would not harm Juarez because it entered downstream from the drinking water. Ross claimed no inhabitants existed for twenty miles, and the current would purify the sewage within two miles.

Mexico called the attitude "criminal and antihumanitarian." It identified a half-dozen communities and ranches affected, and predicted the waste would "convert the salubrious Rio Grande into a death-breeding region."

But while Mexico could be ignored, El Paso could not disregard Ysleta, Texas, twelve miles downstream. Ysleta took no assurances of germ-free sewage in its drinking water, and it halted the disposal with court actions.

A determined Mexico now tried other methods of reducing attrition of its property. Laborers fashioned mattresses of brush and trash, firmly tying and securing them to the river bank with rocks and stakes. In theory these makeshift covers retarded erosion, even occasionally capturing silt and reinforcing the banks.

Wing dams were diversionary mattresses. One end anchored the Mexican bank while the other floated at oblique angles into the stream and was sunk with boulders. The porous construction allowed slow moving water to seep through, but floods ricocheted and undermined the opposite (or American) shore. It amounted to deliberate reverse erosion, a method for regaining portions of the Chamizal.

In early 1897, an awesome flood thundered down the Rio Grande, smashing the wing dams, undermining the mattresses, and breaching Cordova banco, a large bend projecting into El Paso's southeast underbelly. Mattresses and wing dams stacked against bridge pilings. They plugged the shallow channel at Cordova. The brown water backed up and over El Paso, entering buildings as remote as the county courthouse.

After the incursion, El Paso and Juarez severed the neck of Cordova, leaving the international border in the former channel, now usually dry. Cordova became an awkward, inconvenient leg-of-mutton-shaped island of foreign soil protruding into El Paso, its presence an unnatural and ridiculous obstruction to growth.

By now, the Mexican border had come into dispute everywhere along the Rio Grande. The river had changed channels frequently on its way to the Gulf, especially in the delta region of the Lower Rio Grande Valley. So where was the international boundary, exactly? Was it always with the river—or sometimes on dry land?

Since the United States and Mexico had abolished the international boundary commissions during the 1850s, the two countries reluctantly now reinstated the office. They provided authority to investigate disputes and make binding decisions.

The United States appointed Anson Mills as representative. Mexico named Francisco Javier Osorno, an engineer and diplomat. Both were intelligent, competent men.

Across the Rio Grande, Pedro I. García filed suit in the Juarez Primary Court of Claims on November 14, 1895. He demanded a return of 7.82 acres of Chamizal, property disappearing into El Paso because of a shifting river. Additional claimants joined the lawsuit which brought the contested area to six hundred acres. However, the Mexican tribunal lacked authority, so it released transcripts to the International Boundary (Water) Commission. Mills and Osorno would read the evidence, listen to the testimony, and hopefully reach a joint decision. Chamizal deliberations started in April 1896.

Seventy-seven-year-old Jesús Serna of Juarez described the floods of 1854, 1864 and 1868. He worked as a Rio Grande ferryman, and watched the torrents destroy "trees, crops and houses."

Ynocente Ochoa, who had given refuge to Benito Juárez during the French invasion, followed Serna. He recalled the floods of 1858, 1860 and 1864, and described how the water undermined the high Mexican banks. He claimed the noise "seemed like the boom of a cannon, and it was frightful."

Landowner Espiridon Provencio assisted families to higher ground. The river resembled a moving thing, he said, and "up to fifty yards would be washed away at certain points."

Mexico rested while the United States called its first witness. José M. Flores, a Juarez businessman who lived in El Paso and crossed the river daily to work, said the Rio Grande's southward shifts were "imperceptible." Merchant and former mayor Solomon Schutz admitted that the Mexican banks had been worn away, but insisted their erosion had been slow and gradual.

Joseph Magoffin, State National banker and five times El Paso mayor, testified last for Mills. He explained how his father James Magoffin had created Magoffinsville, and how Fort Bliss existed at Magoffinsville for several years. The Rio Grande ravaged Fort Bliss in 1867, the point being that El Paso and Juarez *both* lost land on occasions, the losses usually balancing each other out.

Mexico's final witness was Mariano Samaniego, former Juarez mayor, former Chihuahua governor, landowner, physician and grandfather of El Paso Sheriff Leo Samaniego. He claimed the river had consumed the flowery and productive parts of Juarez. When flood waters got behind or under the mattresses, damage was even more severe. The community often lost 150 acres during one onslaught.

When the testimony ended, Mills and Osorno reviewed engineering reports and prepared final arguments for each other. Osorno made his oral and written statements on July 13 and demanded the entire Chamizal. According to his logic, channel changes were due "to the force of the water's current, not to slow and gradual erosion." No one seriously believes "that a river so inconsistent as the Bravo does its work step by step and degree by degree," he said.

Four days later Mills rebutted. No witness had observed any Mexican land under water, but everyone had watched floods frequently rampaging through El Paso. When a channel changed beds, he said, it left landmarks such as trees and buildings behind. But none of those were in El Paso.

Mills and Osorno failed to agree. Their arguments persuaded no one except themselves. The United States still retained Chamizal.

Three years later in 1909, presidents William Howard Taft and Porfirio Díaz met at the Pass. No records exist of discussions, but after they left, the Chamizal went to arbitration. Anson Mills and Ingeniero Fernando Beltran y Puga (who had replaced Osorno) would continue as judges, but since they were not expected to agree, an arbitrator would make a binding decision. M. Eugene Lafleur came to El Paso from Canada, and he brought a long and honorable background in international law.

The Chamizal Arbitration Commission commenced deliberations in the El Paso Federal Courthouse on May 15, 1911. Both sides dispensed with witnesses and used oral arguments, documents, reports, maps and related records. Thus began a legal struggle not without humor and irony.

Porfirio Díaz abdicated during the proceedings and Francisco Madero assumed the presidency of Mexico. No instructions or messages went to Beltran or his counsel, and neither he nor his associates knew if they had been retained, dismissed or forgotten.

In terms of Mexican participants, few novelists could have chosen a more disparate cast. The commission selected W. J. White as chief counsel and opened itself to charges of unfair influence since White was a close friend of Lafleur. It picked Seymour Thurmond as assistant counsel, an attorney so fond of colorful and long-winded platitudes that Mexican lawyers kept him off the stand to lessen the embarrassment. Finally, there was the former Mexican minister to Washington, Joaquín Casasús. Although he spoke fluent English, and each side had agreed to conduct arguments in English as a courtesy to Lafleur, Casasús unexpectedly insisted on co-equality in Spanish. He gave his best speech in Spanish, the effect being lost when neither Lafleur nor Mills understood it and waited days for a written translation. Two-thirds of the way through the arbitration, Casasús decided he should be in exile, so he did what

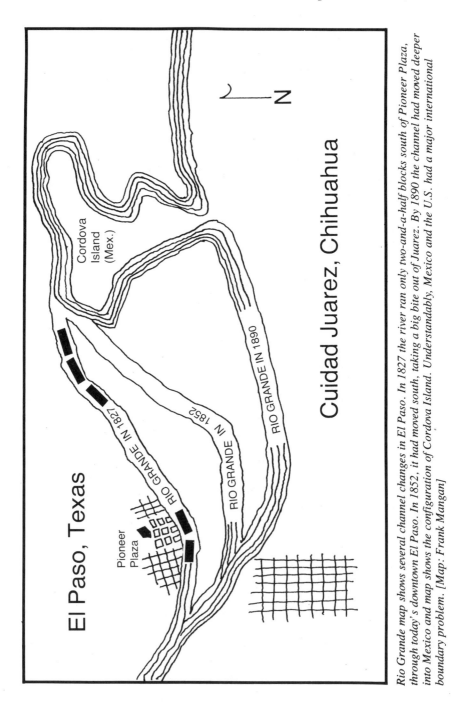

Rio Grande map shows several channel changes in El Paso. In 1827 the river ran only two-and-a-half blocks south of Pioneer Plaza, through today's downtown El Paso. In 1852, it had moved south, taking a big bite out of Juarez. By 1890 the channel had moved deeper into Mexico and map shows the configuration of Cordova Island. Understandably, Mexico and the U.S. had a major international boundary problem. [Map: Frank Mangan]

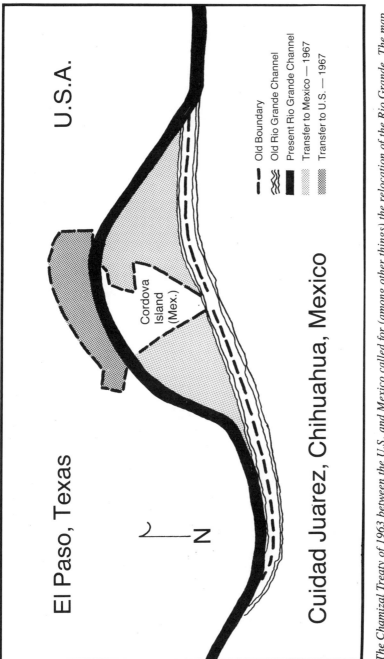

The Chamizal Treaty of 1963 between the U.S. and Mexico called for (among other things) the relocation of the Rio Grande. The map above shows subsequent transfer of disputed property. [Map: Frank Mangan]

wealthy exiles were supposed to do. He went to live in New York.

By contrast the American commission presented practically a perfect case. It was sound, logical, thorough, organized, detailed. It did everything except win.

All three judges responded to six "yes" and "no" answers, the phrasing of each being too complex for citation here. Everybody voted "yes" on one. Mills and Lafleur agreed on two. Lafleur and Beltran agreed on three. Mills ignored two questions he believed irrelevant.

As expected, the American and Mexican positions stayed fixed, so Lafleur exercised his power as arbitrator and awarded Mexico two-thirds of the Chamizal, separating the disputed region along the 1864 river bed. He reasoned that prior changes were slow and gradual, whereas after 1864 the shifts resulted from "rapid erosion." Mexico expressed disappointment but abided by the decision.

Mills rejected the arbitrator's findings, and as America's official spokesman, his veto locked in the United States' position. While to ignore the arbitrator's decision may have been morally suspect according to modern viewpoints, to Mills it was legally and sensibly sound. Mills angrily claimed Lafleur had authority to give away all or none of the Chamizal. He had no authority to divide it. Furthermore, Lafleur made "rapid erosion" the cornerstone of his verdict, the term being meaningless in international law. As for the 1864 river channel, it had never been surveyed. Since its location could not be identified, how could it become the dividing line?

From a historical point of view, Mills probably did the United States and Mexico each a favor. The American government lacked a financial commitment and a sense of social justice necessary to relocate hundreds of Chamizal residents. Lawsuits would have buried the court system.

An arbitrary line in 1911 would have divided streets and parks, jobs and workers, friends and neighbors, families and relatives. Law enforcement, customs and immigration practices would have been maddening. Mexican jurisdiction would have extended to near the very heart of El Paso. During those troublesome years, with revolutionaries capturing Juarez six times in two decades, and with cannon balls still echoing even as the arbitration ran its course, American public opinion would never have permitted Mexican rebels to shoot their way practically to within a few blocks of downtown El Paso. Considering the time and place, the fuzziness of the arbitrator's ruling, Anson Mills had made the correct decision.

For the next half-century the Chamizal issue languished. In 1913,

This 1897 scene looks southeast from a turret atop the first El Paso County Courthouse. Muddy Rio Grande flood waters swirled up from the Cordova banco until they threatened the center of El Paso. [El Paso Public Library]

Secretary of State Philander Knox offered other property in exchange but Mexico refused. The subject clamored for what historian Gladys Gregory called "a decision cutting through the accumulation of historical, legal and technical flotsam . . . ." It needed statesmanship.

By 1962, President John F. Kennedy identified the Chamizal as the outstanding obstacle to improved Mexican relations. Kennedy met with Mexican President López Mateos in Mexico City and they talked of a "complete solution." Two weeks later, Washington advised El Paso authorities of the discussions.

Mexico asked the United States to honor the 1911 arbitration decision and return the land south of the 1864 channel. As that bed had never been surveyed, and its location could only be surmised, the best engineering estimates were that the Americans owed Mexico 437 acres, about two-thirds of a square mile. Mexico called the figure acceptable.

Washington hoped that if it was generous regarding Chamizal, Mexico would be flexible regarding Cordova Island. Mexico had never developed this 287 acre protrusion into El Paso, and had little emotional baggage attached. The Americans realized that after the land transfer, the Rio Grande would need relocating as the international border. To force the river around Cordova Island would require sharp turns, so why not sever Cordova on an east-west line, the United States taking the top half (193 acres). This meant that United States owed Mexico 437 acres for Chamizal, plus 193 acres for Cordova. However, to straighten the Rio Grande even more, the United States gave Mexico 264 acres east of Cordova. By subtracting the 193 acres from the 264 acres, it left an imbalance of 71 acres in favor of Mexico. In order to bring the swap back to an even 437 acres, 71 acres were removed from the Chamizal, making it amount to 366 acres.

As an old saying goes, anything can be proven with figures. The United States cited a flurry of numbers, all meaning the same, but used for different purposes with different audiences. Just keep in mind that Mexico received *exactly* 437.18 acres in the final settlement, nothing more and nothing less. Nevertheless, the most popular quote in El Paso was 630 acres. By subtracting the 193 acres of Cordova Island, the actual sum is back to 437 again. When officials testified before Congress, they generally cited the 437 acres. However, the Chamizal Convention, signed in Mexico on August 29, 1963, and proclaimed in the United States on January 16, 1964, refers to 823 acres. It included 366 acres of Chamizal, the 264 acres east of Cordova which helped straigten the river channel, and the 193 acres of southern Cordova Island which had always belonged to Mexico anyhow and was never in dispute.

Other Areas of Convention agreement were:

1. The center of the Rio Grande would become the international boundary.
2. Neither country would pay the other for land transferred. However, the National Bank of Mexico would purchase structures from the United States that were left standing on the Chamizal portion passing to Mexico.
3. The United States would acquire the Chamizal land and order the evacuation of occupants.
4. The cost of a new river channel lined with concrete would be borne equally by both governments.
5. The existing international bridges would be replaced, and the cost shared.
6. Boundary changes would have no effect on the legal, criminal, or citizenship status of anyone living in, or doing business with, any portion of the exchanged territories.

Ambassador Thomas C. Mann conceived the basic settlement and moved it efficiently through multilayers of government. Along the way,

Chamizal acquired the support of Texas senators John Tower and Ralph Yarborough. When El Paso Congressman Ed Foreman had trouble making up his mind, Richard White replaced him and gave Chamizal his commitment.

American Boundary Commissioner Joseph F. Friedkin coordinated communications between Washington and Mexico City, between El Paso and Juarez, and between El Paso, Austin and Washington. He coalesced diplomatic compromise and engineering practicalities. The tireless Friedkin defended the Chamizal to Congress, and explained exactly how the transaction would be implemented. He argued for appropriations, pointed out how Congress needed to purchase 770 acres. The difference between this and other figures included right-of-way for the new channel, transferring nine miles of railroad track, and relocating federal facilities. Friedkin also pacified the nerves of roughly 300,000 apprehensive El Paso residents who had serious reservations about the "Kennedy give-away."

The El Paso Times and the *El Paso Herald-Post* soothed the unease with vigorous editorials of support. The Chamber of Commerce passed resounding resolutions, and local governments pledged assistance.

Mayor Judson F. Williams, a statesman modest in height but tall in ideas and integrity, deftly guided the Chamizal locally through the shoals of misunderstanding and hostility. The articulate Williams rallied community leaders and persuaded them to speak with one voice.

Local Chamizal adversaries were consistently outflanked and reduced to venting their frustration through letters to the editor. Only Shirley Abbott and Feliciano Hinojosa emerged as spokesmen for the opposition, and even they seemed reluctant. The conservative Abbott insisted to a Senate Foreign Relations Committee that the Chamizal had no legality. Hinojosa, president of the Chamizal Civic Association, wanted specific federal assurances that displaced Americans would receive a just and adequate settlement.

Federal District Judge R. E. Thomason stated repeatedly that residents would get an honest price for land. Thomason had been a former El Paso mayor as well as congressman, and from his bench he asserted that "Uncle Sam doesn't mistreat his citizens. If any of them doesn't obtain a fair value for their property," he thundered, "then come to my court and I'll see they get it."

Judson Williams, in cooperation with Mann and Friedkin, made the fears of Hinojosa and others his own. They obtained a four-point program for El Paso.

1. Adequate compensation for displaced property owners.
2. A six-lane border highway.
3. A national monument park and cultural center on the American portion of Cordova Island.
4. Relocation of the Franklin Canal, preferably underground.

The Franklin Canal started near the present-day Hacienda Cafe and meandered through the city to El Paso's Lower Valley. This irrigation ditch had long been a dangerous eyesore, a filthy stream where young children swam, waded and often drowned. A Chamizal cultural center would add class and beauty to the region. A six-lane border highway would ease El Paso's transportation impediment, and open arteries along the congested edge of the city and the international boundary.

Williams, Mann and Friedkin obtained these concessions primarily by demonstrating what the Chamizal settlement would cost El Paso in lost revenue. The assessed value of El Paso's taxable Chamizal amounted to $9,211,000 in 1960 dollars. Annual revenue losses to the county, state, hospital and school districts ran to $202,000. City and county public investment equaled $10 million. Five hundred and ninety-six residential homes, eighty commercial and industrial structures, and several miles of railroad would be lost. Navarro Elementary School went to Mexico, as did a city dump and Border Patrol administration and detention facilities. Bridges would need replacement.

The Chamizal had benefits too. It amounted to a vast slum clearance, the destruction of tenements so foul that even a Charles Dickens would blanch. While some businesses such as the Mine and Smelter Supply were lost forever, most companies, as well as five thousand Chamizal residents, purchased offices and homes in other parts of the city.

As for Mexico, it did not allocate the Chamizal to squatters, as so many Americans and Mexicans had predicted. Instead it cleared the property, planted 500,000 plants and trees, built a botanical garden, and added a soccer field, a border highway and a major Chamizal memorial.

Anticipated development on the American side moved slowly. The United States gave generously to land owners, paying them not only the value of their property, but replacement and resettlement costs in more affluent areas. It replaced portions, but not all, of the Franklin Canal. The Border Highway was four-lane. The Chamizal National Memorial, built on previous Cordova Island property, was forty percent smaller than anticipated. Chris Fox, State National banker and everyone's "Mr. El

Paso,'' angrily called attention to Mexico's cultural center, and said our own memorial was "for the birds and a constant source of embarrassment." Today's memorial is still underfunded, but due to the brilliant guidance of National Parks Service Superintendent Franklin Smith, it has become a class achievement.

A new Bowie High School arose on Mexico's former Cordova Island. It is a monument to education.

The alien detention facilities never returned. A holding camp near Chamizal for undocumented Mexicans seemed inconsistent with the spirit of neighborly relations, so the City of El Paso donated twenty acres several miles from the border to the Immigration Department.

Only the ultimate swap remained, and the trauma of John F. Kennedy's assassination did not stop presidents Lyndon Baines Johnson and López Mateos from gathering in El Paso at Bowie High School on September 25, 1964. Their ceremony commemorated the reconciliation. On October 28, 1967, Johnson and President Díaz Ordaz greeted each other at the Chamizal Memorial in Juarez and formally transferred lands. All that remained was to lock the Rio Grande inside 4.3 miles of concrete bed, and on December 13, 1968, Johnson and Díaz Ordaz diverted the river into its present channel. That completed a settlement costing the United States in excess of $43 million.

The Chamizal agreement opened up a 1970 treaty with Mexico for "Resolving Boundary Differences," an idea whose time had stalled on account of Chamizal. Furthermore, Chamizal restored injured Mexican pride. After patiently waiting nearly a century for justice, Mexico had prevailed. Today the largest park in Juarez is its Chamizal. Thousands of picnickers daily utilize the shade, the green, soft meadows and the cultural complexes.

El Paso relinquished nearly a square mile of its core. An economic blight had been eradicated, its citizens had financially prospered, transportation facilities had been strengthened, and an old boil sapping economic and cultural vigor had been lanced. Only Fort Bliss, the railroads and possibly Elephant Butte Dam could match the Chamizal's economic impact upon El Paso.

A century old bitterness had in the end brought greater understanding and reconciliation between two nations and two cities. Close neighbors had at least momentarily become close friends.

15

The Legacy of Anson Mills

El Paso continued to be known as Franklin until
1859 when Anson Mills surveyed the townsite,
named the village El Paso, and made an
approved map showing each block in town. A
real estate company was formed to sell lots, and
at this point in history, El Paso finally took on
the appearance of a real town. The 1860 census
listed 428 residents.

Frank Mangan: *El Paso in Pictures*

The imprint, genius and personality of Anson Mills are historically etched upon the Pass of the North. Mills created an El Paso Southwest practically in his own image. He was a first "Mr. El Paso," a civic turning point in himself.

He started life at Thorntown, Indiana on August 31, 1834, entered West Point at the age of nineteen but flunked mathematics. A somewhat chastised Anson then heard of a "promising Mexican settlement" in Texas, a stopover for the Butterfield Overland Stage, a town "eventually to be of some importance." He arrived at Pioneer Plaza at what is now El Paso on the eighth of May, 1858.

Several former West Point classmates at Fort Bliss recommended Mills for district surveyor. He surveyed the military posts of Quitman, Davis, Stockton and Bliss before the Butterfield Company retained him to design and construct the Overland Building. For thirty years it remained the largest structure in town.

Since the village had streets neither straight nor parallel, Mills suggested a development corporation consisting of District Judge J. F. Crosby, J. S. and H. S. Gillett, W. J. Morton, Vincent St. Vrain and William T. "Uncle Billy" Smith. The firm employed Mills to survey a town, and several times Mills drafted a street plan, only to have it refused. On February 28, 1859, the corporation accepted his concept.

Anson Mills named El Paso. The town had been "Ponce's Rancho" from 1827 until 1849 when Benjamin Franklin Coons called it "Franklin" after himself. Abrasive frontier personalities being what they were, Mills denounced Coons as an "undesirable citizen."

In 1858, Anson Mills became the Texas boundary commissioner for surveying the Texas border with New Mexico. However, his cantankerous nature asserted itself, and Mills resigned because of disagreements.

In the meantime, Anson encouraged his brother William Wallace Mills to visit El Paso. W. W. showed the same biting sarcasm as Anson, but he left the community a remarkable memoir, *Forty Years in El Paso,* a frontier saga of civic growth and virulent feuds.

The Mills boys then sent for Emmett, the youngest brother. Together they built "Los Tres Hermanos" (the three brothers), a ranch near Anthony, New Mexico-Texas. It served as a mail station on the Santa Fe Road.

In New Mexico the restless Anson owned several mines and laid out the village of Pinos Altos. He ruefully said the region had the world's greatest supply of gold, but "it had too damned much dirt mixed with it."

Back in El Paso, Anson campaigned for district surveyor, but fell out with former friends and associates of the El Paso Corporation. They considered Mills an abolitionist, a charge so infuriating that on August 6, 1860, Anson left a message on the plaza's newspaper tree:

> I have just been informed that J. S. Gillett, W. J. Morton, and J. R. Sipes stated last night to R. Doane and F. Remy that I was an abolitionist, for the purpose of injuring my character. As I have never cast any other than a Democratic vote or expressed other than Democratic sentiments, I denounce these three above-named persons as willful and malicious lying scoundrels. Sipes and Morton owe me borrowed money for the last two years. I would like to have a settlement. I never asked any one to vote for me as surveyor and I now withdraw my name as a candidate and will not serve if elected.
>
> A. Mills

Morton, Sipes and Gillett flushed and hammered their response firmly to the same ash.

> A certain contemptible "pup," signing himself A. Mills, hav-
> ing publicly published the undersigned as scoundrels, we have
> only to say that he is so notoriously known throughout the entire
> county as a damned black Republican scoundrel, we deem him
> unworthy of further notice.
>   However, we hereby notify this fellow that his insignificance
> will not protect him in the future.
>   W. J. Morton
>   J. R. Sipes
>   John S. Gillett

As the dispute simmered, El Pasoans voted on the issue of secession.
Only the Mills brothers opposed it. Anson in particular displayed in
bold letters, a sign reading NO SEPARATION—Anson Mills.

When the Civil War started, W. W. Mills fled into Paso del Norte
(present-day Juarez) and became a Union spy. Emmett caught the last
stage for California, only to have Apaches led by Mangas Colorado
ambush the coach near Cookes Peak in New Mexico. Indians killed the
passengers after a bristling two-day fight.

Out at Fort Bliss, Anson asked Colonel V. D. Reeve to enter Union
Territory at New Mexico. Reeve refused, surrendered Fort Bliss to the
State of Texas, and marched his men east. Anson left for Washington,
D. C. and enlisted in the Army as a lieutenant.

He had an undistinguished Civil War career. Mills remained in the
Army, rose to major and in 1876, following the Custer debacle at Little
Big Horn, took part in an obscure engagement dubbed the "horsemeat
march." During the Big Horn and Yellowstone Expedition, General
George Crook traveled light and fast to overtake the Sioux. However,
the Army ran out of provisions and ate its horses to survive. Captain
Anson Mills led a detachment for supplies, and unexpectedly encoun-
tered Indians. What followed was the "Charge of Slim Buttes," a gris-
ly, dreary, bitterly cold battle. Several soldiers won the Medal of Honor.
Mills believed he deserved one too, and forty-five years later applied.
The War Department denied it.

The testy Mills put his restless, creative mind into designing a woven-
web ammunition belt. The invention made him wealthy, and he transferred to Fort Bliss, Texas and Fort Selden, New Mexico. Washington

*Always the center of controversy,
Anson Mills surveyed El Paso
and drew its first street map in
1859. He was also a politician,
Indian fighter, developer and
boundary commissioner. El Paso
still bears the imprint of Mills'
name on its history. [Leon Metz
Collection]*

HOTEL VENDOME, EL PASO, TEXAS.

*This 1892 engraving shows mule car (sans mule) on tracks running down what
is now Mills Street. Leafy San Jacinto Plaza is at left, with Hotel Vendome
across Mesa Street. This hotel was to become the site of the Orndorff, Hussmann,
and still later, the Cortez. [El Paso Public Library]*

assigned him as head of the American Boundary Commission, and the War Department promoted him to colonel, authorizing the pay and allowances of an officer on temporary duty off post. The government anticipated a prompt solution to border problems, and when that hope proved naive, the Army retired Anson as a brigadier general. At the age of sixty, he took the oath as American boundary commissioner, swearing in at the Mexican Consulate in El Paso on January 8, 1894.

An initial problem involved "The Island of San Elizario," sometimes known as "Pirate Island" or "The Island." It extended nine miles along the Rio Grande and included thirteen thousand acres. The Rio Grande had jumped its bed so many times that the exact Mexican border had disappeared. Fortunately, the early survey maps still existed, and by August 1896, surveyors had identified and marked the original channel with twenty-one monuments.

Another difficulty involved the *Bosque de Cordova,* a horseshoe curve in the river, the bend rubbing against the southeast underbelly of El Paso. Since the water could not circulate quickly, the river backed up and over El Paso. After the disastrous flood of 1897, boundary commissioners suggested severing the Cordova neck to shorten the flow, increase the grade, and straighten the river. Mills wanted Cordova for the United States, but Mexico retained jurisdiction. Cordova became an island of foreign soil blocking El Paso's growth for over a half-century and causing as much resentment in Texas as the Chamizal did in Mexico.

The Cordova frustration and the Chamizal dispute buffeted the Mills administration. Both involved channel changes in the Rio Grande, and when the Chamizal went to arbitration in 1911, Mills haughtily refused the judgment. Since those days, Anson Mills has been unflatteringly remembered for stonewalling an arbitrator's findings. Yet his commission achievements were considerable and impressive. He advocated two landmark treaties with Mexico. One led to "An Equitable Distribution of the Waters of the Rio Grande" signed in Washington on May 21, 1906. It promised Mexico an annual sixty-thousand acre feet of water from Elephant Butte Dam.

The other involved bancos. A banco was a bend in the Rio Grande similar to the one at Cordova. When the river formed an oxbow, the channels often shifted during high water and those movements obscured the international line.

Largely through the efforts of Anson Mills, both countries signed a 1905 treaty for the "Elimination of Bancos." Engineers severed the banco necks, and those curves protruding into Texas fell to the jurisdiction of the United States. The ones in Mexico belonged to that country. By 1970, 241 bancos were eliminated and thirty thousand acres had changed hands.

The boundary commissions went into near limbo during the 1910-1920 Mexican Revolution, and President Theodore Roosevelt decided on a change of administrators. A campaign started to force Anson Mills from office as Colorado Senator Charles Spalding Thomas accused him of paying his assistants too much money. Mills of course knew what the politicians wanted, and he resigned on July 1, 1914. Even that did not save him from a 1915 congressional drubbing. During a hearing that consumed sixty-five pages, the committee found no wrongdoing.

Anson turned his attention to the Mills Building in El Paso. He and J. F. Crosby had built the Grand Central Hotel in 1883, and after it burned, Anson erected the Mills Building on the site, the tallest concrete monolith in the world. Construction began in 1910, with the exterior completed in 1911. Not all the interior floors were finished until 1916. Today the Mills Building, often known as the Electric Building, is no longer the highest structure in town. But it remains *the* landmark of El Paso.

Anson Mills, the surveyor, engineer, Indian fighter, politician, inventor, developer, businessman, military officer, feisty individualist and boundary commissioner died on November 5, 1924 at the age of ninety. The Army buried him with honors in Arlington National Cemetery.

Before his death, he completed *My Story*. While it described early El Paso and cited important details about American relations with Mexico, it was an organizational maze, a tribute to an ego larger than the Mills Building. It lacked W. W.'s flair for literary elegance.

Although Anson Mills had the personality of a falling brick, that should not diminish his accomplishments nor corrode his dreams. Some of his lesser known but significant passions deserve a mention.

Mills believed in constant progress. He called war the most "cruel, barbarous and destructive" of all man's evils. He stood stoutly and proudly for woman suffrage, marching in the parades and publicly applauding the leaders. He supported prohibition, acknowledging that he was an occasional drinking-man himself, but that he could handle it and most others could not. Acts of racial prejudice dismayed him, and he suggested that the world would never find true peace and happiness until all men could live like brothers.

Anson Mills loved his family, his country and El Paso. When you see the city he named and helped build, you see his monument.

Acknowledgments

My thanks to Art Roberts, Director of the El Paso Chamber of Commerce, and to Russell Autry, Editor, *El Paso Magazine*. Thanks to *El Paso Magazine* staffers Heidi Beginski, managing editor; Brenda Castaneda, editorial assistant; Leroy Smith, associate publisher; Antonio Castro, artist; Joe Pando, art director.

I want to thank Frank and Judy Mangan who *are* Mangan Books. They have never failed to reach out their hand.

Also, much appreciation goes to William Schilling, Martha Peterson and Teresa Irvin, expert proofreaders; National Parks Service Superintendent Frank Smith at the Chamizal National Monument and his associates Richard Razo, Bernie Valencia, Fred Erhard and Joe Birdwell; Mary Sarber of the El Paso Public Library; Boundary Commissioner Joseph Friedkin and his assistant, Robert Ybarra; geologist William Strain; Loretta Martin of the El Paso Museum of Art; historian Millard McKinney; artists Suzanne Bilodeau and Fred Carter; photographers Cletis Reaves and Jose Andow.

Finally I want to thank my wife Cheryl who edits my manuscripts and puts up with my long hours at the typewriter.

LCM

Sources

CHAPTER 1

Big River

Information is found in a scattering of sources, including material obtained by the International Boundary and Water Commission. Paul Horgan's two volume history, *Great River* (Rinehart: New York, 1954), is of course the standard guide to the Rio Grande. One might also consult *Rio Grande*, by Harvey Fergusson (Tudor: New York, 1945), and *Dividing the Waters: A Century of Controversy between the United States and Mexico* by Norris Hundley, Jr. (California: Berkeley, 1966). William S. Strain, Professor Emeritus at UT El Paso, furnished most of the geological data, notably "Bolson Integration in the Texas-Chihuahua Border Region," and "Late Cenozoic Bolson Integration in the Chihuahua Tectonic Belt." Both papers were read in the Nov. 4-6, 1970 symposium at Midland, Texas, the discussions sponsored by the West Texas Geological Society.

CHAPTER 2

La Toma and the Right Arm of God

The best on Oñate still remains the classic two volume, *Oñate: Colonizer of New Mexico*, edited by George P. Hammond (New Mexico: Albuquerque, 1953). Additional El Paso information can be found in C. L. Sonnichsen's *Pass of the North* (Texas Western Press: El Paso, 1968), and *Four Centuries at the Pass*, edited by Dr. W. H. Timmons (City of El Paso Arts Resources Department, 1980).

CHAPTER 3

Muskets at the Pass

Considerable background can be found in *Fort Bliss: An Illustrated History,* by Leon C. Metz & Millard G. McKinney (Mangan Books: El Paso, 1981). Also see *El Paso in Pictures,* by Frank Mangan (Mangan Books, El Paso, 1971); *The Garrison at Fort Bliss, 1849-1916,* by M. H. Thomlinson (Hertzog & Resler: El Paso, 1945); and *Musket, Saber & Missile: A History of Fort Bliss,* by Major Richard K. McMaster (Richard K. McMaster: El Paso, 1963). Two other strong sources of early Fort Bliss are Allan W. Sandstrum's

Fort Bliss: The Frontier Years, Thesis for the Graduate Division, June 1962, Texas Western College, El Paso; and *Password,* the official quarterly of the El Paso County Historical Society.

CHAPTER 4

When El Paso Left New Mexico and Joined Texas

The commissioners court minutes are in the El Paso County Courthouse. Other documents are in the Texas State Archives in Austin. A book having more than superficial coverage is *Robert Simpson Neighbors and the Texas Frontier, 1836–1859,* by Kenneth F. Neighbours (Texian Press: Waco, 1975). An important recent article is "Military Influence on the Texas-New Mexico Boundary Settlement," by Thomas S. Edrington, *New Mexico Historical Review,* (Vol. 59, No. 4).

CHAPTER 5

El Paso and the War in the West

There is no better record of the Civil War than the multi-volume series, *War of the Rebellion.* Even so, much of the New Mexico records have been extracted and are available in *Confederate Victories in the Southwest,* edited by the Publishers (Horn & Wallace: Albuquerque, 1961). Historical buffs will also want the two publications by Martin Hardwick Hall, *Sibley's New Mexico Campaign* (Texas: Austin, 1960), and *The Confederate Army in New Mexico* (Presidial Press: Austin, 1978). Darlis Miller wrote *The California Column in New Mexico* (New Mexico: Albuquerque, 1982). Two books of personal memoirs are, *Bloody Trails on the Rio Grande,* by Alonzo Ferdinand Ickis (The Old West Publishing Co.: Denver, 1958), and *Rebels on the Rio Grande: The Civil War Journals of A. B. Peticolas,* edited by Don E. Alberts (New Mexico: Albuquerque, 1984).

CHAPTER 6

Blood and Salt

C. L. Sonnichsen's *The El Paso Salt War* (Carl Hertzog and the Texas Western Press: El Paso,

1961), is the most complete written account of this struggle that we will likely ever get. A few stray Salt War articles are found in *Password,* El Paso County Historical Society quarterly. For the congressional inquiry, read *El Paso Troubles in Texas,* House Executive Document No. 93, 45th Cong., 2nd Session.

CHAPTER 7

Lonesome Whistle

Edward A. Leonard's *Rails at the Pass of the North* offers a fairly comprehensive outline of railroads in El Paso (Southwestern Study, Monograph No. 63, Texas Western Press: El Paso, 1981). *Pass of the North,* by C. L. Sonnichsen (Texas Western Press: El Paso, 1968) also mentions the railroad in some detail. Several articles are in *Password,* El Paso County Historical Society quarterly.

CHAPTER 8

The Case of the Stolen County Seat

There is some information in commissioners court minutes in the El Paso County Courthouse. However, *The El Paso Times, El Paso Herald* and the *El Paso Lone Star* are the best known sources of information available.

CHAPTER 9

The Struggle for Law and Order

Dallas Stoudenmire: El Paso Marshal, by Leon C. Metz (Oklahoma: Norman, 1979), is the only full-length biography of Stoudenmire in print. Fred R. Egloff has added new wrinkles to the "Four Dead in Five Seconds" shootout with a fine biography, *El Paso Lawman: G. W. Campbell* (Creative Publishing: College Station, 1982). C. L. Sonnichsen's *Pass of the North* (Texas Western Press: El Paso, 1968) has considerable information on El Paso's wild days. Additional material is in *The El Paso Times,* the *El Paso Herald* and the *El Paso Lone Star.* Those interested in political affairs should examine the City Council Minutes, available in typescript at the El Paso Public Library.

CHAPTER 10

Shady Ladies

The Gentlemen's Club: The Story of Prostitution in El Paso, by H. Gordon Frost (Mangan Books: El Paso, 1983) is the only comprehensive and outstanding history. However, C. L. Sonnichsen also includes the subject in his *Pass of the North* (Texas Western Press: El Paso, 1968.)

CHAPTER 11

When Fort Bliss Almost Moved to New Mexico

Fort Bliss: An Illustrated History, by Leon C. Metz and Millard G. McKinney (Mangan Books: El Paso, 1981) is perhaps the most comprehensive of items relating to the post. Of strong importance is a Dissertation in History for Texas Tech University (August, 1977), entitled "Sword and Plowshare: the Symbiotic Development of Fort Bliss and El Paso, Texas," by Garna Loy Christian. For an excellent article, read George Ruhlen's, "The Genesis of Fort Bliss," *Password* (Vol. XIX, No. 4).

CHAPTER 12

The Battle of Juarez

There are several written accounts of this battle, including articles found in local El Paso newspapers and in *Password,* El Paso County Historical Society quarterly. The superior books are *El Paso in Pictures,* by Frank Mangan (Mangan Books: El Paso, 1971); *Pass of the North,* by C. L. Sonnichsen (Texas Western Press: El Paso, 1968); *Bullets, Bottles and Gardenias,* by Timothy G. Turner (South-West Press: Dallas, 1935); *Gringo Doctor,* by I. J. Bush (Caxton: Caldwell, 1939); and *Frontier Newspaper: The El Paso Times,* by John Middagh (Texas Western Press: El Paso, 1958). While dissertations and theses have been written, one of the most comprehensive is *Border Revolution: The Mexican Revolution in the Ciudad Juarez-El Paso Area, 1906-1915,* by Richard M. Estrada, Thesis for the master of Arts, December, 1975 UT El Paso.

CHAPTER 13

The Elephant Butte Saga

The Elephant Butte dispute involves primary research. The records are in the International Boundary and Water Commission, the National Archives, and the Department of Reclamation. The *El Paso Herald* and *The El Paso Times* are filled with news regarding the controversy. Information is also available in *My Story,* by Anson Mills (Press of Byron S. Adams: Washington, D. C., 1921), and in *History of the Development of Irrigation in the El Paso Valley,* by Alice M. White, Thesis for the Graduate School, May 1950, Texas Western College.

CHAPTER 14

Restless River, Disputed Land

A complete list of Chamizal sources would take

a book in itself, and important items would still be missed. *The El Paso Times* and the *El Paso Herald-Post* contain informative articles. Government documents number in the dozens, and the International Boundary and Water Commission has more. The El Paso Planning Department stores materials. Chamizal treasures abound in Mexican archives and newspapers. The Texas State Archives has important papers. Numerous individuals have private collections. Yet, there exists no book-length history of Chamizal. Gladys Gregory came close with *The Chamizal Settlement,* a Southwestern Study of Texas Western Press in El Paso, Texas, 1963. She also wrote a dissertation for the University of Texas at Austin, 1937, entitled "El Chamizal: A Boundary Problem between the United States and Mexico." Another well-written Dissertation in History (Texas Tech, 1945) is "The Chamizal Dispute: An Exercise in Arbitration, 1845-1945," by Kenneth D. Yeilding. Readers might be interested in *Restless River,* by Jerry E. Mueller (Texas Western Press: El Paso, 1975). A few significant short studies are "The United States and Mexico: Sources of Conflict," by Sam J. Moore & Cesar Sepulveda *(Southwestern Law Journal,* Vol. 17, No. 1), and "El Chamizal: A Century Old Boundary Dispute," by James E. Hill, Jr. *(Geographical Review,* Vol. 55, No. 4).

CHAPTER 15

The Legacy of Anson Mills

The best source for this man's life is his own account, *My Story,* by Anson Mills (Press of Byron S. Adams: Washington, D. C., 1921). His brother's book, *Forty Years in El Paso,* by W. W. Mills (Carl Hertzog: El Paso, 1963) has considerable insight. Indian fighting experiences are recounted in, *Slim Buttes, 1876: An Episode of the Great Sioux War,* by Jerome A. Greene (Oklahoma, Norman, 1982). The International Boundary and Water Commission has the Mills' records as boundary commissioner. Local newspapers also are full of information.

Index